# WJEC GCSE
# MATHEMATICS
## Foundation Homework Book

### Wyn Brice, Linda Mason and Tony Timbrell

**Second Edition**

HODDER
EDUCATION
AN HACHETTE UK COMPANY

The Publishers would like to thank WJEC for permission to reproduce past examination questions throughout this book.

This material has been endorsed by WJEC and offers high quality support for the delivery of WJEC qualifications. While this material has been through a WJEC quality assurance process, all responsibility for the content remains with the publisher.

Hachette UK's policy is to use papers that are natural, renewable and recyclable products and made from wood grown in sustainable forests. The logging and manufacturing processes are expected to conform to the environmental regulations of the country of origin.

Orders: please contact Bookpoint Ltd, 130 Milton Park, Abingdon, Oxon OX14 4SB. Telephone: (44) 01235 827720. Fax: (44) 01235 400454. Lines are open 9.00–5.00, Monday to Saturday, with a 24-hour message answering service. Visit our website at www.hoddereducation.co.uk

First published in 2006 by
Hodder Education, an Hachette UK Company,
338 Euston Road
London NW1 3BH

This second edition published in 2010.

Impression number    5  4  3  2
Year                        2014 2013  2012

Cover photo © Imagestate Media
Typeset in 10/12pt Times New Roman PS by Pantek Media, Maidstone, Kent
Printed by CPI Group (UK) Ltd, Croydon CR0 4YY

A catalogue record for this title is available from the British Library

ISBN 978 1444 115291

# → CONTENTS

# → INTRODUCTION

This book contains exercises designed to be used for the Foundation tier of GCSE Mathematics. It is particularly aimed at WJEC's Linear and Unitised Specifications and each exercise matches one in the WJEC GCSE Mathematics Foundation Student's Book.

In the Homework Book, the corresponding exercises have the same number and end in H. Thus, for example, if you have been working on Interpreting graphs in class and used Exercise 25.1, then the homework exercise is 25.1H. The homework exercises cover the same mathematics. Some chapters also have exercises corresponding to the review exercises in the textbook.

Some questions are intended to be completed without a calculator, just as in the textbook. These are shown with a non-calculator icon in the same way. Doing these questions without a calculator is vital preparation for the non-calculator section of the examination papers.

These homework exercises provide extra practice and are also in a smaller book to carry home! If you have understood the topics, you should be able to tackle these exercises confidently as they are no harder than those you have done in class and in some cases may be a little easier. See if you agree.

You will find the answers to this homework book in the Foundation Teacher's Website.

# 1 → INTEGERS, POWERS AND ROOTS 1

##  EXERCISE 1.1H

**1** Work out these.
   a) 46 + 32        b) 68 + 35
   c) 86 + 59        d) 178 + 26
   e) 185 + 232      f) 188 + 346

**2** Work out these.
   a) 87 − 42        b) 72 − 26
   c) 72 − 39        d) 239 − 87
   e) 273 − 148      f) 634 − 276

**3** Work out these.
   a) 32 × 4         b) 28 × 6
   c) 38 × 3         d) 49 × 8
   e) 135 × 7        f) 278 × 5

**4** Work out these.
   a) 69 ÷ 3         b) 54 ÷ 3
   c) 96 ÷ 6         d) 92 ÷ 4
   e) 165 ÷ 5        f) 232 ÷ 4

**5** Meena bought a top for £24, a pair of jeans for £37 and a belt for £9. What was the total cost?

**6** Karim had £50.
He bought two CDs for £13 each. How much did he have left?

**7** Liz bought eight pens at 38p each. What was the total cost in pence?

**8** Will organises a disco. The cost of hiring the hall and the disc jockey is £468. How many £6 tickets does he need to sell to cover the cost?

## EXERCISE 1.2H

**1** List the following.
   a) The multiples of 9 less than 100
   b) The multiples of 12 less than 100

**2** Use your answers to question **1** to list the common multiples of 9 and 12 less than 100.

**3** Look at these numbers.

   4, 7, 9, 16, 18, 21, 25, 30, 42

   a) Which have 2 as a factor?
   b) Which have 3 as a factor?
   c) Which have 7 as a factor?

**4** List the following.
   a) The multiples of 20 less than 130
   b) The multiples of 25 less than 130

**5** Use your answers to question **4** to find a common multiple of 20 and 25 less than 130.

**6** List the following.
   a) The factors of 20
   b) The factors of 36

**7** Use your answers to question **6** to list the common factors of 20 and 36.

**8** List the following.
   a) The factors of 60
   b) The factors of 24

**9** Use your answers to question **8** to list the common factors of 60 and 24.

10 Round these numbers to the nearest 1000.
   a) 32 300        b) 203 900
   c) 6600          d) 243 497
   e) 3 503 776

11 Round these numbers to the nearest 100.
   a) 8392          b) 21 830
   c) 354           d) 756 982
   e) 7032

12 Here are some newspaper headlines. Round the numbers so that they have more impact.
   a) Blues win with a majority of 7832!
   b) £2 127 836 wasted by 'red tape'!
   c) Moody goes to Real for €34 632 578!
   d) Number passing goes up by 12 364!

# EXERCISE 1.3H

1 Work out these.
   a) $71 \times 10$          b) $84 \times 100$
   c) $26 \times 1000$        d) $402 \times 100$
   e) $78 \times 10\,000$     f) $80 \times 100$
   g) $617 \times 1000$       h) $2800 \times 100$
   i) $140 \times 1000$       j) $84 \times 10\,000$
   k) $974 \times 100\,000$   l) $76 \times 1\,000\,000$

2 Work out these.
   a) $590 \div 10$
   b) $29\,000 \div 100$
   c) $648\,000 \div 1000$
   d) $92\,000 \div 100$
   e) $9\,200\,000 \div 1000$
   f) $789\,000 \div 10$
   g) $458\,200 \div 100$
   h) $8\,400\,000 \div 100$
   i) $71\,000\,000 \div 10\,000$

3 Work out these.
   a) $40 \times 30$          b) $60 \times 90$
   c) $80 \times 300$         d) $400 \times 400$
   e) $700 \times 50$         f) $60 \times 50$
   g) $800 \times 4000$       h) $500 \times 200$
   i) $900 \times 8000$       j) $6000 \times 2000$
   k) $60\,000 \times 30$     l) $7000 \times 9000$

4 Work out these.
   a) $53 \times 20$          b) $63 \times 40$
   c) $165 \times 50$         d) $73 \times 400$
   e) $82 \times 700$         f) $59 \times 600$
   g) $537 \times 800$        h) $96 \times 3000$

5 Work out these.
   a) $72 \times 24$          b) $64 \times 36$
   c) $71 \times 96$          d) $59 \times 23$
   e) $88 \times 39$          f) $252 \times 47$
   g) $348 \times 65$         h) $546 \times 83$
   i) $792 \times 96$         j) $85 \times 384$

6 a) How many centimetres are there in 589 metres?
   b) Change 4900 centimetres into metres.

7 1 hectare is 10 000 square metres. How many square metres is 63 hectares?

8 Jeans cost £30 per pair. How much will eight pairs cost?

9 A sales representative drives 400 miles per working day. How far does he drive in a year if he works on 235 days?

10 138 people attended a dinner dance. If the tickets were £26 each, what was the total amount they paid?

# EXERCISE 1.4H

 **1** Work out these without your calculator.
  **a)** $1^2$    **b)** $8^2$    **c)** $2^4$
  **d)** $40^2$    **e)** $70^2$    **f)** $80^2$
  **g)** $300^2$    **h)** $500^2$    **i)** $600^2$
  **j)** $110^2$

 **2** Use your calculator to work out these.
  **a)** $18^2$    **b)** $34^2$    **c)** $52^2$
  **d)** $78^2$    **e)** $86^2$    **f)** $47^2$
  **g)** $57^2$    **h)** $240^2$    **i)** $389^2$
  **j)** $643^2$

 **3** Use your calculator to work out these.
  **a)** $7^3$        **b)** $8^3$
  **c)** $12^3$        **d)** $18^3$
  **e)** $34^3$        **f)** $48^3$
  **g)** $56^3$        **h)** $231^3$

 **4** Use your calculator to work out these.
  **a)** $\sqrt{256}$        **b)** $\sqrt{441}$
  **c)** $\sqrt{576}$        **d)** $\sqrt{1024}$
  **e)** $\sqrt{3969}$        **f)** $\sqrt{5476}$
  **g)** $\sqrt{3364}$        **h)** $\sqrt{7921}$

 **5** Work out these without your calculator.
  **a)** $\sqrt{1600}$    **b)** $\sqrt{4900}$    **c)** $\sqrt{8100}$
  **d)** $\sqrt{10\,000}$    **e)** $\sqrt{90\,000}$

# EXERCISE 1.5H

**1** Work out these.
  **a)** $-3$ add 5
  **b)** $-8$ add 4
  **c)** 7 subtract 11

**2** The temperature is $-7°C$.
  Find the new temperature after
  **a)** a rise of $4°C$.
  **b)** a rise of $10°C$.
  **c)** a fall of $6°C$.

**3** Find the difference in temperature between
  **a)** $8°C$ and $26°C$.
  **b)** $-3°C$ and $12°C$.
  **c)** $-23°C$ and $-11°C$.

**4** Arrange these numbers in order, smallest first.
  **a)** $2, -6, 5, -4$
  **b)** $7, -5, 0, -8$
  **c)** $-2, 6, -7, -8, 9, 3$

**5** An aircraft flies at 15 000 m where the outside temperature is $-70°C$.
  When the aircraft lands, the outside temperature is $21°C$.
  What is the difference between these temperatures?

# 2 → FRACTIONS

 **EXERCISE 2.1H**

1  What fraction is
   a)  4 of 12?        b)  18 of 24?
   c)  9 of 15?        d)  14 of 21?
   e)  18 of 36?       f)  £20 of £80?
   g)  7 cm of 56 cm?  h)  22 g of 77 g?
   Write the fractions in their lowest
   terms.

2  Copy and complete the following.
   a)  $\dfrac{1}{3} = \dfrac{\square}{6} = \dfrac{3}{\square} = \dfrac{10}{12} = \dfrac{\square}{300}$

   b)  $\dfrac{1}{7} = \dfrac{2}{\square} = \dfrac{\square}{21} = \dfrac{4}{\square} = \dfrac{\square}{70} = \dfrac{100}{\square}$

3  Copy and complete the following.
   a)  $\dfrac{3}{5} = \dfrac{\square}{15}$       b)  $\dfrac{10}{18} = \dfrac{5}{\square}$
   c)  $\dfrac{1}{2} = \dfrac{\square}{24}$       d)  $\dfrac{50}{70} = \dfrac{5}{\square}$
   e)  $\dfrac{12}{22} = \dfrac{\square}{11}$     f)  $\dfrac{4}{7} = \dfrac{12}{\square}$
   g)  $\dfrac{5}{11} = \dfrac{\square}{66}$      h)  $\dfrac{3}{27} = \dfrac{1}{\square}$
   i)  $\dfrac{2}{9} = \dfrac{\square}{36}$       j)  $\dfrac{4}{13} = \dfrac{\square}{39}$
   k)  $\dfrac{25}{45} = \dfrac{5}{\square}$      l)  $\dfrac{63}{70} = \dfrac{\square}{10}$

4  Express these fractions in their lowest
   terms.
   a)  $\dfrac{10}{14}$   b)  $\dfrac{3}{18}$    c)  $\dfrac{16}{20}$   d)  $\dfrac{18}{30}$
   e)  $\dfrac{21}{35}$   f)  $\dfrac{30}{50}$   g)  $\dfrac{24}{36}$   h)  $\dfrac{32}{56}$
   i)  $\dfrac{4}{52}$    j)  $\dfrac{70}{140}$  k)  $\dfrac{20}{160}$  l)  $\dfrac{200}{1000}$
   m)  $\dfrac{18}{54}$   n)  $\dfrac{42}{56}$   o)  $\dfrac{60}{72}$   p)  $\dfrac{75}{125}$

 **EXERCISE 2.2H**

1  Find $\frac{1}{3}$ of these quantities.
   a)  30        b)  36        c)  69
   d)  £90       e)  £15

2  Find $\frac{1}{5}$ of these quantities.
   a)  35        b)  55        c)  90
   d)  £140      e)  36 m

3  Find $\frac{3}{4}$ of these quantities.
   a)  36        b)  60        c)  100
   d)  £68       e)  £180

4  Find $\frac{5}{6}$ of these quantities.
   a)  60        b)  36        c)  90
   d)  48 cm     e)  £150

5  Faheem receives £24 for his birthday.
   He saves $\frac{1}{4}$ of it.
   How much does he save?

6  Each week Abigail earns £20.
   She spends $\frac{1}{5}$ of it on sweets and drinks
   and saves $\frac{3}{10}$ of it.
   a)  How much does she spend on
       sweets and drinks?
   b)  How much does she save?

**7** The maths budget is £800. $\frac{3}{5}$ is spent on textbooks. How much is left?

**8** There are 180 students in year 9. $\frac{4}{9}$ of them come to school by bus. How many come by bus?

**9** A school has 720 students. $\frac{5}{8}$ of them have school dinners. How many students have school dinners?

**10** Which is the larger, a $\frac{3}{8}$ share of £160 or a $\frac{4}{5}$ share of £80? Show your working.

# EXERCISE 2.3H

**1** Work out these. Where possible cancel the fractions to their lowest terms.

a) $\frac{1}{6} \times 5$   b) $\frac{1}{9} \times 4$   c) $\frac{2}{5} \times 2$

d) $3 \times \frac{2}{9}$   e) $4 \times \frac{1}{12}$

**2** Change these improper fractions to mixed numbers.

a) $\frac{11}{4}$   b) $\frac{12}{5}$   c) $\frac{14}{3}$   d) $\frac{21}{2}$

e) $\frac{23}{4}$   f) $\frac{23}{6}$   g) $\frac{33}{8}$   h) $\frac{12}{11}$

i) $\frac{19}{4}$   j) $\frac{79}{10}$

**3** Work out these.
Write your answers first as improper fractions, then as mixed numbers. Where possible cancel the fractions to their lowest terms.

a) $\frac{1}{2} \times 11$   b) $\frac{3}{5} \times 4$   c) $\frac{3}{7} \times 4$

d) $6 \times \frac{5}{7}$   e) $4 \times \frac{4}{9}$   f) $\frac{5}{8} \times 4$

g) $\frac{3}{10} \times 6$   h) $10 \times \frac{3}{8}$   i) $7 \times \frac{3}{5}$

j) $\frac{5}{11} \times 7$   k) $\frac{5}{6} \times 8$   l) $9 \times \frac{9}{10}$

m) $10 \times \frac{5}{8}$   n) $\frac{5}{12} \times 8$   o) $7 \times \frac{5}{21}$

# 3 → DECIMALS

##  EXERCISE 3.1H

1  Write in words the place value of the digit 8 in each of these numbers.
   a)  800          b)  0.8          c)  8000
   d)  8.74         e)  0.028

2  Write these numbers as decimals.
   a)  $\frac{9}{10}$       b)  $8\frac{3}{10}$       c)  $\frac{7}{100}$
   d)  $61\frac{23}{100}$       e)  $\frac{183}{1000}$

3  Write these decimals as fractions or mixed numbers (whole numbers and fractions) in their lowest terms.
   a)  0.4          b)  5.1          c)  27.5
   d)  0.25         e)  1.13

4  Write all these amounts in pounds. Then arrange them in order, smallest first.
   £13.84  82p  £4.09  £0.08  12p  £5.79

5  Write these numbers in order, largest first.
   0.816   8.61   0.068   1.806   60.1

6  Use the fact that there are 1000 millilitres in a litre to write these capacities in litres.
   a)  250 ml       b)  1500 ml
   c)  185 ml       d)  5 ml
   e)  2250 ml

7  Write these lengths in centimetres.
   a)  1.2 m        b)  84 mm
   c)  3.85 m       d)  56 mm
   e)  7 mm

8  Write these lengths in order, smallest first.
   7.3 cm  0.61 m  83 mm  2.08 m  48.1 cm

9  Draw a grid to show that $\frac{2}{5} = \frac{4}{10} = 0.4$.

10 Write these fractions as decimals.
   a)  $\frac{7}{10}$       b)  $\frac{1}{2}$       c)  $\frac{4}{5}$
   d)  $\frac{3}{4}$       e)  $\frac{13}{100}$

##  EXERCISE 3.2H

1  Work out these.
   a)  $\begin{array}{r} 3.87 \\ +9.15 \\ \hline \end{array}$  b)  $\begin{array}{r} 38.43 \\ +59.12 \\ \hline \end{array}$

   c)  $\begin{array}{r} 41.53 \\ +67.42 \\ \hline \end{array}$  d)  $\begin{array}{r} 16.19 \\ +\ 8.34 \\ \hline \end{array}$

   e)  $\begin{array}{r} 36.84 \\ +53.92 \\ \hline \end{array}$  f)  $\begin{array}{r} 137.58 \\ +273.16 \\ \hline \end{array}$

2  Work out these.
   a)  $\begin{array}{r} 19.28 \\ -\ 6.25 \\ \hline \end{array}$  b)  $\begin{array}{r} 47.16 \\ -15.42 \\ \hline \end{array}$

   c)  $\begin{array}{r} 253.80 \\ -\ 81.47 \\ \hline \end{array}$  d)  $\begin{array}{r} 17.84 \\ -\ 8.13 \\ \hline \end{array}$

   e)  $\begin{array}{r} 57.42 \\ -23.51 \\ \hline \end{array}$  f)  $\begin{array}{r} 721.58 \\ -236.82 \\ \hline \end{array}$

**3** Work out these.
   **a)** £3.95 + 82p + £1.57
   **b)** £15.21 + 77p + £3.42 + 61p
   **c)** £63.84 + 90p +£8.51 +
   £91.20 + 47p
   **d)** £6.25 + 42p + 87p + £63.20

**4** Find the cost of six DVDs at £13.45
   each.

**5** In the javelin, Amina throws 52.15 m
   and Raj throws 46.47 m.
   Find the difference between the
   lengths of their throws.

**6** The times for the first and last places
   in a show-jumping event were
   47.82 seconds and 53.19 seconds.
   Find the difference between these
   times.

**7** Melissa buys three identical bags of
   carrots as shown.

WEIGHT | PRICE
0.450 KG | 99p

   **a)** What is the total weight?
   **b)** What is the total cost?

**8** Find the cost of 3 kg of onions at
   £0.72 per kilogram.

**9** Work out these. Give your answers in
   the larger unit.
   **a)** 7.3 m + 87 cm + 6.1 m
   **b)** 5.2 m + 54 cm + 3.85 m + 76 cm
   **c)** 6.1 m − 278 cm
   **d)** 4.5 m − 57 cm
   **e)** 12.1 cm − 7 mm

**10** Work out these. Where applicable,
   give your answers in the larger unit.
   **a)** 650 g + 1.7 kg + 56 g + 2.1 kg
   **b)** 3.7 kg + 450 g − 1.5 kg
   **c)** 1.4 kg − 586 g
   **d)** 2 litres − 730 ml
   **e)** 3 × 0.58 litres

**11** Holly buys two scarves at £8.45 each
   and one pair of shoes at £35.99.
   How much change does she get from
   £60?

**12** Dean buys two newspapers at 55p each
   and three magazines at £1.20 each.
   How much change does he get from
   £10?

**13** Work out these.
   **a)** 6 × 0.4       **b)** 0.2 × 7
   **c)** 5 × 0.3       **d)** 0.8 × 9
   **e)** 0.4 × 0.1     **f)** 0.7 × 0.8
   **g)** 50 × 0.7      **h)** 0.3 × 80
   **i)** 0.4 × 0.3     **j)** 0.6 × 0.1
   **k)** $(0.7)^2$     **l)** $(0.2)^2$

# 4 → PERCENTAGES

 **EXERCISE 4.1H**

1 Change these percentages to fractions. Write your answers in their lowest terms.
   a) 45%          b) 85%
   c) 4%           d) 130%

2 Change these percentages to decimals.
   a) 18%    b) 26%    c) 92%
   d) 8%     e) 42%    f) 3%
   g) 12%    h) 1%     i) 170%
   j) 350%   k) 5%     l) 14.5%

3 Change these decimals to percentages.
   a) 0.73    b) 0.28    c) 0.06
   d) 0.235   e) 1.68

4 Change these fractions to percentages.
   a) $\frac{3}{10}$    b) $\frac{4}{5}$    c) $\frac{13}{20}$
   d) $\frac{7}{25}$    e) $\frac{18}{40}$

5 a) Write $\frac{1}{4}$ as a decimal.
   b) Write 0.5 as a fraction.
   c) Write 30% as a decimal.
   d) Write $\frac{1}{4}$, 0.5 and 30% in descending order.

6 a) Write $\frac{2}{5}$ as a decimal.
   b) Write 0.25 as a fraction.
   c) Write 10% as a decimal.
   d) Write $\frac{2}{5}$, 0.25 and 10% in order of size, starting with the smallest first.

7 a) (i)   Write $\frac{1}{2}$ as a decimal.
      (ii)  Write 0.4 as a fraction.
      (iii) Write 60% as a decimal.
      (iv)  Write $\frac{1}{2}$, 0.4 and 60% in ascending order.
   b) Shade 75% of the following shape.

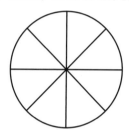

8 Showing all your working, find which of the quantities 0.8, $\frac{17}{20}$ and 84% is
   a) the smallest, b) the largest.

9 Showing all your working, find which of the quantities $\frac{9}{20}$, 40% and 0.42 is
   a) the smallest. b) the largest.

# EXERCISE 4.2H

 Do not use your calculator for questions 1 to 6.

1 Find 25% of £84.

2 Find 60% of 35 kg.

3 Find 15% of £70.

4 James borrowed £80 000 to buy a house and paid 7% interest in the first year. Calculate the interest.

**5** 30% of the students in Year 7 came from one primary school.
There are 220 students in Year 7. How many came from that primary school?

**6** 15% of Mr and Mrs Thompson's Council Tax is used to pay for police, fire service and civil defence. Mr and Mrs Thompson's Council tax bill is £1200. How much goes to pay for police, fire service and civil defence?

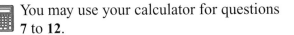 You may use your calculator for questions **7** to **12**.

**7** Find 19% of £36.

**8** Find 37% of 240 metres.

**9** Find 108% of £64.

**10** 92% of the seats at a concert were sold out after one week.
There were 32 000 seats available. How many were sold out in the first week?

**11** Sarah pays 6% of her earnings into a pension fund.
She earns £1450 per month. How much does she pay into the pension fund each month?

**12** Michael changes £350 into euros. The bank charges him 2.5% commission. How much is the commission?

# EXERCISE 4.3H

Do not use your calculator for questions **1** to **6**.

**1** Increase £700 by these percentages.
a) 40%    b) 35%
c) 70%    d) 21%

**2** Decrease £520 by these percentages.
a) 70%    b) 25%
c) 6%    d) 20%

**3** Michelle earns £16 000 per year. She receives a salary increase of 3%. Find her new salary.

**4** A company cuts its wage bill by 15%. Its wage bill before the cut was £4 600 000.
What was the wage bill after the cut?

**5** A furniture shop is having a sale.

**40% off**

Copy and complete the table to find the sale price of these articles.

| Item | Original price (£) | Reduction (£) | Sale price (£) |
|---|---|---|---|
| Bookcase | 180 | | |
| Dining table and chairs | 840 | | |
| Sofa | 440 | | |
| Display unit | 260 | | |

**6** Amy earns £360 per week. She pays 11% national insurance and 15% income tax.
Calculate Amy's weekly take-home pay.

You may use your calculator for questions 7 to **12**.

**7** Increase £84 by these percentages.

   **a)** 14%    **b)** 36%

   **c)** 9%    **d)** 72%

**8** Decrease £428 by these percentages.

   **a)** 23%    **b)** 37%

   **c)** 7%    **d)** 69%

**9** The value of a car fell by 12% in the first year.
   It cost £16 800 when new.
   What was its value after one year?

**10** 8% more people passed an examination in 2010 than in 2009.
   6400 passed in 2009.
   How many passed in 2010?

**11** In 1971 there were 902 000 births in the UK. By 1981 the birth rate had fallen by 19%.
   Calculate the number of births in 1981. Give your answer to the nearest thousand.

**12** An antique increased in value by 180% in five years. It was worth £240 at the start of the five years.
   What was it worth at the end of the five years?

# EXERCISE 4.4H

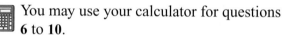 Do not use your calculator for questions 1 to **5**.

**1** Calculate £4 as a percentage of £50.

**2** Calculate 8 metres as a percentage of 40 metres.

**3** Calculate 90p as a percentage of £3.

**4** Graeme earns £50 per week. He receives a pay increase of £2 per week. Calculate his pay increase as a percentage of £50.

**5** A computer originally costing £600 is reduced by £90.
   Calculate the reduction as a percentage of the original price.

You may use your calculator for questions 6 to **10**.

**6** Calculate £64 as a percentage of £400.

**7** Calculate 180 kg as a percentage of 400 kg.

**8** The number of houses built in a town in 2008 was 480. This increased by 168 in 2009.
   Find the increase as a percentage of 480.

**9** The value of an investment fell from £4800 in 2003 to £4200 in 2008.
   Find the reduction as a percentage of £4800.

**10** In 2010 the national minimum wage was raised from £5.80 to £5.93.
   Calculate the increase as a percentage of £5.80.
   Give your answer to the nearest whole number.

# 5 → MENTAL METHODS 1

 ## EXERCISE 5.1H

Work out these.

| | | | |
|---|---|---|---|
| 1 | 12 + 20 | 2 | 51 + 30 |
| 3 | 44 + 70 | 4 | 59 + 30 |
| 5 | 67 + 70 | 6 | 12 + 23 |
| 7 | 21 + 36 | 8 | 13 + 45 |
| 9 | 23 + 47 | 10 | 24 + 37 |
| 11 | 52 + 36 | 12 | 26 + 69 |
| 13 | 41 + 23 | 14 | 49 + 36 |
| 15 | 36 + 56 | 16 | 47 + 81 |
| 17 | 53 + 67 | 18 | 43 + 88 |
| 19 | 94 + 58 | 20 | 49 + 63 |

 ## EXERCISE 5.2H

Work out these.

| | | | |
|---|---|---|---|
| 1 | 50 − 20 | 2 | 80 − 20 |
| 3 | 46 − 30 | 4 | 59 − 40 |
| 5 | 121 − 60 | 6 | 39 − 15 |
| 7 | 33 − 8 | 8 | 88 − 27 |
| 9 | 38 − 25 | 10 | 74 − 53 |
| 11 | 83 − 19 | 12 | 72 − 39 |
| 13 | 44 − 28 | 14 | 86 − 18 |
| 15 | 67 − 29 | 16 | 100 − 41 |
| 17 | 90 − 33 | 18 | 94 − 27 |
| 19 | 100 − 35 | 20 | 46 − 19 |

 ## EXERCISE 5.3H

How many do you need to add to
1  25 to make 100?    2  63 to make 100?
3  27 to make 80?     4  42 to make 65?

5  51 to make 93?    6  37 to make 69?
7  29 to make 78?    8  46 to make 92?
9  25 to make 81?    10  56 to make 83?

 ## EXERCISE 5.4H

Work out these.

| | | | | | |
|---|---|---|---|---|---|
| 1 | 2 × 3 | 2 | 3 × 2 | 3 | 7 × 6 |
| 4 | 6 × 7 | 5 | 7 × 2 | 6 | 4 × 8 |
| 7 | 9 × 9 | 8 | 5 × 4 | 9 | 3 × 3 |
| 10 | 8 × 3 | 11 | 9 × 6 | 12 | 5 × 8 |
| 13 | 3 × 7 | 14 | 6 × 4 | 15 | 9 × 10 |
| 16 | 8 × 8 | 17 | 10 × 3 | 18 | 5 × 7 |

 ## EXERCISE 5.5H

Work out these.

| | | | | | |
|---|---|---|---|---|---|
| 1 | 8 ÷ 2 | 2 | $\frac{24}{3}$ | 3 | 20 ÷ 5 |
| 4 | 24 ÷ 4 | 5 | 35 ÷ 5 | 6 | 7)14 |
| 7 | 18 ÷ 6 | 8 | 42 ÷ 7 | 9 | 21 ÷ 3 |
| 10 | $\frac{72}{9}$ | 11 | 30 ÷ 6 | 12 | $\frac{72}{8}$ |
| 13 | 48 ÷ 6 | 14 | 7)28 | 15 | 54 ÷ 9 |
| 16 | 2)12 | 17 | 27 ÷ 3 | 18 | 60 ÷ 6 |

## EXERCISE 5.6H

Estimate the value of each of these.

| | | | | | |
|---|---|---|---|---|---|
| 1 | $\sqrt{19}$ | 2 | $\sqrt{41}$ | 3 | $\sqrt{74}$ |
| 4 | $\sqrt{10}$ | 5 | $\sqrt{26}$ | 6 | $\sqrt{83}$ |
| 7 | $\sqrt{97}$ | 8 | $\sqrt{51}$ | 9 | $\sqrt{42}$ |

## EXERCISE 5.7H

1   Round these numbers to the nearest whole number.
   a)   24.3            b)   561.5
   c)   81.2            d)   417.6
   e)   81.91           f)   128.43
   g)   39.8            h)   627.203
   i)   5.32            j)   4.57

2   Round these numbers to 1 decimal place.
   a)   2.37            b)   8.24
   c)   9.45            d)   12.6666
   e)   8.912           f)   12.87
   g)   9.624           h)   7.465
   i)   6.1919          j)   1.95

3   Round these numbers to 2 decimal places.
   a)   2.837           b)   1.624
   c)   5.465           d)   5.1919
   e)   1.2345          f)   7.381
   g)   6.247           h)   7.318
   i)   7.904           j)   9.595

4   Round these numbers to 1 significant figure.
   a)   64              b)   372
   c)   9414            d)   98
   e)   9012            f)   54 217
   g)   2594            h)   45 092
   i)   1631            j)   1871.32

5   A man won £3 871 242 in a lottery. How much was this correct to 1 significant figure?

## EXERCISE 5.8H

Work out these.

1   $3 - 5$            2   $5 - 2$
3   $7 - 5$            4   $4 - 6$
5   $3 - 4$            6   $4 + 3$
7   $-1 + 3$           8   $-3 + 3$
9   $-4 + 1$           10  $2 + 1$
11  $-2 - 3$           12  $-7 + 6$
13  $-3 + 2$           14  $-6 - 5$
15  $-3 - 2$           16  $-3 + (-4)$
17  $4 + (-5)$         18  $-4 - (-3)$
19  $-2 + (-1)$        20  $-6 - (-4)$

## EXERCISE 5.9H

Work out these.

1   $5 - 3 + 2 - 1$
2   $3 + 3 - 5 - 2$
3   $2 + 3 + 2 - 5$
4   $6 - 4 - 3 + 2$
5   $-5 + 3 - 2 + 2$
6   $5 - 2 - 3 - 1$
7   $8 - 3 + 2 - 6$
8   $4 - 3 - 5 - 1 + 4 + 1$
9   $6 + 2 + 1 - 4 - 3 + 3$
10  $-2 - 4 + 2 + 8 - 6 - 2$

## REVIEW EXERCISE 5H

1   a)   Write down, in figures, the number seven thousand and ninety seven.
    b)   47   42   63   29   53   27   46
         (i)   Write down two of the above numbers which add up to 100.
         (ii)  Write down two of the above numbers whose difference is 13.
    c)   Write 57 259
         (i)   to the nearest 100.
         (ii)  to the nearest 1000.

**2 a)** Write down, in figures, the number seven thousand and eighty five.

**b) (i)** Work out $236 + 67$.
**(ii)** Work out $853 - 348$.

**c)** Estimate the value of $48 \times 7.9$.

**3 a)** Write down, in figures, the number eight thousand and thirty seven.

**b)** Find the sum of 273 and 358.

**c)** Find the difference between 458 and 439.

**d)** Write 5838
**(i)** correct to the nearest 10.
**(ii)** correct to the nearest 100.

**e)** Andrew uses each of the digits 2 5 6 9 to make up four-digit numbers.
**(i)** What is the smallest **even** number that he can make?
**(ii)** What is the largest **odd** number that he can make?

**f)** Showing your working find an estimate for $49.8 \times 4.9$.

**4 a)** Write down, in figures, the number six thousand seven hundred and eight.

**b)**
| 70 | 29 | 47 | 36 | 24 |
|----|----|----|----|----|
| 52 | 28 | 63 | 53 | |

From the list of numbers shown above, write down
**(i)** two numbers which add up to 100.
**(ii)** two numbers which have a difference of 46.

**c)** Using all of the digits 2 9 5 7 write down the largest four-digit number.

**d)** What is the value of the 6 in the number 7863?

**e)** The number 537 is multiplied by 10. What is the value of the 3 in the answer?

**f)** The number 6780 is divided by 10. What is the value of the 8 in the answer?

**5 a) (i)** A television cost one thousand and eighty pounds. Write down the cost of the television in figures.
**(ii)** Arnold wins £12 000 000. Write this amount in words.

**b) (i)** What must be added to 67 to make 94?
**(ii)** What must be taken away from 105 to leave 48?

**c)**
| 912 | 921 | 936 | 953 |
|-----|-----|-----|-----|
| 901 | 987 | 934 | 978 |

From the above list of numbers write down
**(i)** the smallest number.
**(ii)** the largest number.

**d)** Showing all your working, estimate the value of $198.7 \times 10.2$.

**6 a)** Mark buys a suit and an overcoat. The suit costs £135 and the overcoat costs £129. Find the total cost of the suit and the overcoat.

**b)** Sian buys a dress. The cost of the dress is £124. Sian uses seven twenty pound notes to pay for the dress. How much change should Sian be given?

**c)** Mary wants to buy a new camera.
She goes to five shops and notes
the price of the same camera in
each shop.
The prices are:
£278   £281   £298   £273   £297
Write down
**(i)** the lowest price of the camera.
**(ii)** the highest price of the camera.

7   Only using numbers taken from the
following list,

  2     5     9     12     17
18     32     38     42

**a)** Write down the two numbers
which add up to 49.
**b)** Write down the two numbers
whose difference is 29.
**c)** Write down the two numbers
which when multiplied together
give an answer of 84.
**d)** When 63 is divided by a number
the answer is 7.
Write down the number.

8   Use the fact that $86 \times 73 = 6278$ to
write down the answers to the
following
**a)** $8.6 \times 73 =$
**b)** $860 \times 7.3 =$
**c)** $6278 \div 73 =$

# 6 → USING A CALCULATOR

## EXERCISE 6.1H

**1** Work out these squares.

a) $4.3^2$      b) $7.2^2$
c) $56^2$      d) $419^2$
e) $0.74^2$      f) $0.82^2$
g) $0.09^2$      h) $3.2^2$
i) $4.71^2$      j) $63.8^2$

**2** Work out these square roots.

a) $\sqrt{14.44}$      b) $\sqrt{68.89}$
c) $\sqrt{3.61}$      d) $\sqrt{219.04}$
e) $\sqrt{3844}$      f) $\sqrt{0.1156}$
g) $\sqrt{0.5776}$      h) $\sqrt{0.0324}$
i) $\sqrt{10.3041}$      j) $\sqrt{0.007\,225}$

**3** Work out these square roots. Give your answers correct to 2 decimal places.

a) $\sqrt{45.3}$      b) $\sqrt{74.8}$
c) $\sqrt{44}$      d) $\sqrt{827}$
e) $\sqrt{5632}$      f) $\sqrt{0.468}$
g) $\sqrt{0.4}$      h) $\sqrt{56\,846}$
i) $\sqrt{0.408}$      j) $\sqrt{0.063}$

**4** The area of a square is 720 cm². Find the length of its side.
Give your answer correct to 1 decimal place.

## EXERCISE 6.2H

Work out these on your calculator without writing down the answers to the middle stages.
If the answers are not exact, give them correct to 3 decimal places.

**1** $(7.3 + 3.2) \div 4.8$

**2** $(134 - 43) \div 35$

**3** $(8.2 - 3.6) \times 5.4$

**4** $\sqrt{(17.3 + 16.8)}$

**5** $\sqrt{(68.7 - 2.3^2)}$

**6** $(7.3 - 2.6)^2$

**7** $7.3^2 - 2.6^2$

**8** $16.8 \div (5.2 - 1.9)$

**9** $5.8 \times (1.9 + 7.3)$

**10** $\sqrt{(28.6 - 9.7)}$

**11** $\sqrt{(26.2 \div 3.8)}$

**12** $34.9 \div (2.8 + 5.3)$

# 7 → INTEGERS, POWERS AND ROOTS 2

## EXERCISE 7.1H

Write each of these numbers as a product of its prime factors.

| | | | |
|---|---|---|---|
| **1** | 14 | **2** | 16 |
| **3** | 28 | **4** | 35 |
| **5** | 42 | **6** | 49 |
| **7** | 108 | **8** | 156 |
| **9** | 225 | **10** | 424 |

## EXERCISE 7.2H

For each of these pairs of numbers
- write the numbers as products of their prime factors.
- state the highest common factor.
- state the lowest common multiple.

| | | | |
|---|---|---|---|
| **1** | 6 and 8 | **2** | 8 and 18 |
| **3** | 15 and 25 | **4** | 36 and 48 |
| **5** | 25 and 55 | **6** | 33 and 55 |
| **7** | 54 and 72 | **8** | 30 and 40 |
| **9** | 45 and 63 | **10** | 24 and 50 |

##  EXERCISE 7.3H

Work out these.

| | | | |
|---|---|---|---|
| **1** | $2 \times 3$ | **2** | $-5 \times 8$ |
| **3** | $-6 \times -2$ | **4** | $-4 \times 6$ |
| **5** | $5 \times -7$ | **6** | $-3 \times 7$ |
| **7** | $-4 \times -5$ | **8** | $28 \div -7$ |
| **9** | $-25 \div 5$ | **10** | $-20 \div 4$ |
| **11** | $24 \div 6$ | **12** | $-15 \div -3$ |
| **13** | $-35 \div 7$ | **14** | $64 \div -8$ |
| **15** | $27 \div -9$ | **16** | $3 \times 6 \div -9$ |

**17** $-42 \div -7 \times -3$

**18** $5 \times 6 \div -10$

**19** $-9 \times 4 \div -6$

**20** $-5 \times 6 \times -4 \div -8$

## EXERCISE 7.4H

 Do not use your calculator for questions **1** and **2**.

**1** Write down the value of each of these.
- **a)** $1^2$
- **b)** $13^2$
- **c)** $\sqrt{64}$
- **d)** $\sqrt{196}$
- **e)** $3^3$
- **f)** $5^3$
- **g)** $\sqrt[3]{8}$
- **h)** $\sqrt[3]{27}$

**2** A cube has sides of length 4 cm. What is its volume?

You may use your calculator for questions **3** to **7**.

**3** Find the square of each of these numbers.
- **a)** 20
- **b)** 42
- **c)** 5.1
- **d)** 60
- **e)** 0.9

**4** Find the cube of each of these numbers.
- **a)** 7
- **b)** 3.5
- **c)** 9.4
- **d)** 20
- **e)** 100

**5** Find the square root of each of these numbers.
Where necessary, give your answer correct to 2 decimal places.
- **a)** 900
- **b)** 75
- **c)** 284
- **d)** 31 684
- **e)** 40 401

**6** Find the cube root of each of these numbers.
Where necessary, give your answer correct to 2 decimal places.
**a)** 729 **b)** 144 **c)** 9.261
**d)** 4848 **e)** 100 000

**7** A square has an area of 80 cm$^2$.
What is the length of one side? Give your answer correct to 2 decimal places.

# EXERCISE 7.5H

**1** Write these in simpler form using indices.
**a)** $2 \times 2 \times 2 \times 2 \times 2 \times 2$
**b)** $7 \times 7 \times 7 \times 7$
**c)** $2 \times 2 \times 3 \times 3 \times 3 \times 3 \times 5 \times 5 \times 5$

Hint: Write the different numbers separately.

**2** Work out these giving your answers in index form.
**a)** $2^2 \times 2^4$ **b)** $3^6 \times 3^2$
**c)** $4^2 \times 4^3$ **d)** $5^6 \times 5$

**3** Work out these giving the answers in index form.
**a)** $5^5 \div 5^2$ **b)** $7^8 \div 7^2$
**c)** $2^6 \div 2^4$ **d)** $3^7 \div 3^3$

**4** Work out these giving your answers in index form.
**a)** $\dfrac{2^5 \times 2^4}{2^3}$ **b)** $\dfrac{3^7}{3^5 \times 3^2}$
**c)** $\dfrac{5^5 \times 5^4}{5^2 \times 5^3}$ **d)** $\dfrac{7^5 \times 7^2}{7^2 \times 7^4}$

**5 a)** Write each of these numbers as a product of its prime factors.
**(i)** 36 **(ii)** 49 **(iii)** 64
**(iv)** 100 **(v)** 324

**b)** All the numbers in part **a)** are square numbers. Write down what you notice about all the powers (indices) in part **a)**.

**6** Write 50 as a product of its prime factors. What is the least number that 50 needs to be multiplied by so that the result is a square number?

**7 a)** Write each of these numbers as a product of its prime factors.
**(i)** 12 **(ii)** 27 **(iii)** 60
**(iv)** 75 **(v)** 112

**b)** For each number in parts **a) (i)** to **(v)**, find the least number it needs to be multiplied by so that the result is a square number.

# EXERCISE 7.6H

Do not use your calculator for questions **1** to **3**.

**1** Write down the reciprocal of each of these numbers.
**a)** 4 **b)** 9 **c)** 65

**2** Write down the numbers of which these are the reciprocals.
**a)** $\frac{1}{6}$ **b)** $\frac{1}{10}$ **c)** $\frac{1}{25}$

**3** Find the reciprocal of each of these numbers.
Give your answers as fractions or mixed numbers.
**a)** $\frac{3}{5}$ **b)** $\frac{4}{9}$ **c)** $2\frac{2}{5}$

You may use your calculator for question **4**.

**4** Find the reciprocal of each of these numbers.
Give your answers as decimals.
**a)** 25 **b)** 0.2 **c)** 6.4

# 8 → FRACTIONS, DECIMALS AND PERCENTAGES

## EXERCISE 8.1H

1. For each pair of fractions
   - find the lowest common denominator.
   - state which is the bigger fraction.

   **a)** $\frac{7}{8}$ or $\frac{3}{4}$    **b)** $\frac{5}{9}$ or $\frac{7}{11}$    **c)** $\frac{1}{6}$ or $\frac{3}{20}$

2. Work out these.

   **a)** $\frac{3}{7} + \frac{2}{7}$    **b)** $\frac{7}{15} + \frac{4}{15}$

   **c)** $\frac{8}{11} - \frac{3}{11}$    **d)** $\frac{11}{17} - \frac{8}{17}$

   **e)** $\frac{7}{16} + \frac{3}{16}$    **f)** $\frac{7}{9} + \frac{4}{9}$

   **g)** $\frac{7}{12} - \frac{5}{12}$    **h)** $\frac{8}{11} + \frac{5}{11}$

   **i)** $2\frac{4}{7} + 3\frac{1}{7}$    **j)** $4\frac{5}{6} - 1\frac{1}{6}$

   **k)** $5\frac{9}{13} - \frac{4}{13}$    **l)** $4\frac{3}{8} - 1\frac{5}{8}$

3. Work out these.

   **a)** $\frac{2}{9} + \frac{1}{3}$    **b)** $\frac{7}{12} + \frac{1}{4}$

   **c)** $\frac{3}{4} - \frac{1}{10}$    **d)** $\frac{13}{16} - \frac{3}{8}$

   **e)** $\frac{7}{8} + \frac{1}{3}$    **f)** $\frac{4}{5} + \frac{5}{6}$

   **g)** $\frac{7}{12} - \frac{1}{8}$    **h)** $\frac{9}{20} + \frac{3}{4}$

   **i)** $\frac{7}{11} + \frac{3}{5}$    **j)** $\frac{7}{12} + \frac{7}{10}$

   **k)** $\frac{7}{8} - \frac{1}{6}$    **l)** $\frac{7}{15} - \frac{3}{20}$

4. Work out these.

   **a)** $4\frac{1}{4} + 3\frac{1}{3}$    **b)** $6\frac{8}{9} - 1\frac{2}{3}$

   **c)** $5\frac{3}{8} + \frac{1}{4}$    **d)** $5\frac{11}{16} - 2\frac{1}{8}$

   **e)** $2\frac{5}{6} + 3\frac{1}{4}$    **f)** $6\frac{8}{9} - 2\frac{1}{6}$

   **g)** $3\frac{5}{8} + 4\frac{7}{10}$    **h)** $5\frac{7}{11} - 5\frac{1}{3}$

   **i)** $4\frac{3}{4} + 3\frac{2}{7}$    **j)** $6\frac{1}{4} - 2\frac{2}{3}$

   **k)** $7\frac{1}{9} - 2\frac{1}{2}$    **l)** $5\frac{3}{10} - 4\frac{4}{5}$

## EXERCISE 8.2H

1. Change these mixed numbers to improper fractions.

   **a)** $4\frac{3}{5}$   **b)** $6\frac{1}{4}$   **c)** $3\frac{4}{7}$   **d)** $1\frac{5}{9}$

   **e)** $4\frac{5}{6}$   **f)** $7\frac{3}{10}$   **g)** $4\frac{7}{8}$

2. Work out these.
   Write your answers as proper fractions or mixed numbers in their lowest terms.

   **a)** $\frac{3}{7} \times 5$    **b)** $\frac{5}{9} \times 6$    **c)** $\frac{3}{5} \div 4$

   **d)** $6 \times \frac{5}{11}$    **e)** $\frac{2}{9} \div 4$    **f)** $9 \div \frac{3}{8}$

3. Work out these.
   Write your answers as proper fractions or mixed numbers in their lowest terms.

   **a)** $\frac{2}{3} \times \frac{5}{7}$    **b)** $\frac{1}{8} \times \frac{5}{6}$

   **c)** $\frac{7}{9} \times \frac{2}{5}$    **d)** $\frac{5}{8} \div \frac{3}{4}$

   **e)** $\frac{3}{8} \div \frac{1}{3}$    **f)** $\frac{4}{9} \times \frac{5}{11}$

   **g)** $\frac{6}{7} \times \frac{1}{8}$    **h)** $\frac{7}{15} \div \frac{2}{3}$

   **i)** $\frac{7}{12} \times \frac{3}{8}$    **j)** $\frac{9}{16} \div \frac{7}{12}$

   **k)** $\frac{7}{10} \div \frac{5}{12}$    **l)** $\frac{7}{30} \times \frac{10}{21}$

4. Work out these.
   Write your answers as proper fractions or mixed numbers in their lowest terms.

   **a)** $4\frac{3}{4} \times 1\frac{7}{9}$    **b)** $3\frac{2}{3} \times \frac{1}{5}$

   **c)** $4\frac{2}{5} \div 2\frac{4}{5}$    **d)** $1\frac{3}{11} \div 3\frac{1}{2}$

   **e)** $4\frac{1}{2} \times 3\frac{2}{3}$    **f)** $3\frac{5}{9} \div 2\frac{2}{3}$

   **g)** $3\frac{2}{7} \times 1\frac{5}{9}$    **h)** $2\frac{5}{8} \div 1\frac{5}{6}$

   **i)** $1\frac{7}{15} \times 12\frac{1}{2}$    **j)** $5\frac{3}{5} \div 1\frac{3}{4}$

   **k)** $6\frac{2}{9} \times 2\frac{1}{8}$    **l)** $7\frac{1}{2} \div 2\frac{3}{5}$

**EXERCISE 8.3H**

**1** Work out these.

a) $\frac{3}{4} + \frac{1}{6}$  b) $\frac{5}{8} - \frac{2}{7}$

c) $\frac{5}{9} \times \frac{3}{8}$  d) $\frac{7}{16} \div \frac{5}{12}$

e) $1\frac{4}{5} + 2\frac{3}{4}$  f) $6\frac{3}{7} - 2\frac{1}{3}$

g) $5\frac{3}{5} \times 4$  h) $4\frac{5}{9} \div 1\frac{1}{6}$

**2** Write these fractions in their lowest terms.

a) $\frac{40}{125}$  b) $\frac{28}{49}$  c) $\frac{72}{192}$

d) $\frac{225}{350}$  e) $\frac{17}{153}$

**3** Write these improper fractions as mixed numbers.

a) $\frac{120}{72}$  b) $\frac{150}{13}$  c) $\frac{86}{19}$

d) $\frac{192}{54}$  e) $\frac{302}{17}$

**4** Calculate
a) the perimeter of this rectangle.
b) the area of this rectangle.

$5\frac{3}{5}$ cm

$2\frac{1}{4}$ cm

 **EXERCISE 8.4H**

**1** Change each of these fractions to a decimal.
If necessary, give your answer to 3 decimal places.

a) $\frac{7}{8}$  b) $\frac{7}{100}$

c) $\frac{5}{9}$  d) $\frac{2}{11}$

**2** State whether each of these fractions gives a recurring or a terminating decimal.
Give a reason for each answer.

a) $\frac{3}{4}$  b) $\frac{5}{6}$  c) $\frac{5}{11}$

d) $\frac{2}{25}$  e) $\frac{7}{32}$

**3** a) Find the recurring decimal equivalent to $\frac{3}{101}$.
b) How many digits are there in the repeating pattern?

**EXERCISE 8.5H**

Work out these. As far as possible, write down only your final answer.

1  $3.4 + 6.1$      2  $4.3 + 3.6$
3  $5.8 - 2.3$      4  $7.9 - 4.4$
5  $3.7 + 2.6$      6  $5.8 + 3.4$
7  $7.2 - 0.9$      8  $5.4 - 3.5$
9  $8.6 + 2.7$      10  $6.9 + 4.6$
11  $6.7 - 5.8$     12  $6.3 - 2.9$

**EXERCISE 8.6H**

**1** Work out these.

a) $5 \times 0.4$  b) $0.6 \times 8$
c) $4 \times 0.7$  d) $0.9 \times 6$
e) $0.7 \times 0.3$  f) $0.9 \times 0.4$
g) $50 \times 0.7$  h) $0.4 \times 80$
i) $0.7 \times 0.1$  j) $0.4 \times 0.2$
k) $(0.8)^2$  l) $(0.2)^2$

**2** Work out these.

a) $6 \div 0.3$  b) $4.8 \div 0.2$
c) $2.4 \div 0.6$  d) $7.2 \div 0.4$
e) $33 \div 1.1$  f) $60 \div 1.5$
g) $12 \div 0.4$  h) $35 \div 0.7$
i) $64 \div 0.8$  j) $32 \div 0.2$
k) $2.17 \div 0.7$  l) $47.5 \div 0.5$

**3** Work out these.

a) $3.6 \times 1.4$    b) $5.8 \times 2.6$
c) $8.1 \times 4.3$    d) $6.5 \times 3.2$
e) $74 \times 1.7$    f) $64 \times 3.8$
g) $2.9 \times 7.6$    h) $11.4 \times 3.2$
i) $25.2 \times 0.8$    j) $2.67 \times 0.9$
k) $8.45 \times 1.2$    l) $7.26 \times 2.4$

**4** Work out these.

a) $23.6 \div 0.4$    b) $23.4 \div 0.8$
c) $18.2 \div 0.7$    d) $31.2 \div 0.6$
e) $42.3 \div 0.9$    f) $75.6 \div 1.2$
g) $5.28 \div 0.3$    h) $7.56 \div 0.7$
i) $63.2 \div 0.2$    j) $6.27 \div 1.1$
k) $3.51 \div 1.3$    l) $8.19 \div 1.3$

# EXERCISE 8.7H

**1** Write down the multiplier that will increase an amount by the following percentages.

a) 17%    b) 30%    c) 73%
d) 6%    e) 1%    f) 12.5%
g) 160%

**2** Write down the multiplier that will decrease an amount by the following percentages.

a) 13%    b) 40%    c) 35%
d) 8%    e) 4%    f) 27%
g) 15.5%

**3** Mrs Green bought an antique for £200. She later sold it at 250% profit. What did she sell it for?

**4** Jane earns £14 500 per year. She receives an increase of 2%. Find her new salary.

**5** In a sale, all items are reduced by 20%. Shamir bought a computer in the sale.

Its original price was £490. What was its sale price?

**6** Graham invested £3500 at 4% compound interest. What was the investment worth at the end of 5 years? Give your answer to the nearest pound.

**7** A car decreased in value by 11% per year. If it cost £16 500 new, what was it worth after 4 years? Give your answer to a suitable degree of accuracy.

**8** In a certain country, the population rose by 5% every year from 2004 to 2009. If the population was 26.5 million in 2004, what was the population in 2009? Give your answer in millions to the nearest 0.1 of a million.

**9** Jane invested £4500 with compound interest for 3 years. She could receive either 3% interest every 6 months or 6% interest every year. Which should Jane choose and how much more will she receive?

**10** Prices went up by 2% in 2007, 3% in 2008 and 2.5% in 2009. If an item cost £32 at the start of 2007 what did it cost at the end of 2009?

# 9 → RATIO AND PROPORTION

 ## EXERCISE 9.1H

1   Write each of these ratios in its lowest terms.
   a)  8 : 6
   b)  20 : 50
   c)  35 : 55
   d)  8 : 24 : 32
   e)  15 : 25 : 20

2   Write each of these ratios in its lowest terms.
   a)  200 g : 500 g
   b)  60p : £3
   c)  1 minute : 25 seconds
   d)  2 m : 80 cm
   e)  500 g : 3 kg

3   A bar of brass contains 400 g of copper and 200 g of zinc.
   Write the ratio of copper to zinc in its lowest terms.

4   Teri, Jannae and Abi receive £200, £350 and £450 respectively as their dividends in a joint investment.
   Write the ratio of their dividends in its lowest terms.

5   Three saucepans hold 500 ml, 1 litre and 2.5 litres respectively.
   Write the ratio of their capacities in its lowest terms.

## EXERCISE 9.2H

1   Write each of these ratios in the form $1 : n$.
   a)  2 : 10        b)  5 : 30
   c)  2 : 9         d)  4 : 9
   e)  50 g : 30 g   f)  15p : £3
   g)  25 cm : 6 m   h)  20 : 7
   i)  4 mm : 1 km

2   On a map, a distance of 12 mm represents a distance of 3 km.
   What is the scale of the map in the form $1 : n$?

3   A picture is enlarged on a photocopier from 25 mm wide to 15 cm wide.
   What is the ratio of the picture to the enlargement in the form $1 : n$?

## EXERCISE 9.3H

1   A photo is enlarged in the ratio 1 : 5.
   a)  The length of the small photo is 15 cm.
       What is the length of the large photo?
   b)  The width of the large photo is 45 cm.
       What is the width of the small photo?

2   To make a dressing for her lawn,
    Rupinder mixes loam and sand in the
    ratio 1 : 3.
    a)  How much sand should she mix
        with two buckets of loam?
    b)  How much loam should she mix
        with 15 buckets of sand?

3   To make mortar, Fred mixes 1 part
    cement with 5 parts sand.
    a)  How much sand does he mix with
        500 g of cement?
    b)  How much cement does he mix
        with 4.5 kg of sand?

4   A rectangular picture is 6 cm wide.
    It is enlarged in the ratio 1 : 4.
    How wide is the enlargement?

5   The Michelin motoring atlas of France
    has a scale of 1 cm to 2 km.
    a)  On the map, the distance between
        Metz and Nancy is 25 cm.
        How far is the actual distance
        between the two towns?
    b)  The actual distance between Caen
        and Falaise is 33 km.
        How far is this on the map?

6   Graham is making pastry.
    To make enough for five people he
    uses 300 g of flour.
    How much flour should he use to
    make enough for eight people?

7   To make a solution of a chemical, a
    scientist mixes 2 parts chemical with
    25 parts water.
    a)  How much water should he mix
        with 10 ml of chemical?
    b)  How much chemical should he mix
        with 1 litre of water?

8   The ratio of the sides of two rectangles
    is 2 : 5.
    a)  The length of the small rectangle is
        4 cm.
        How long is the big rectangle?
    b)  The width of the big rectangle is
        7.5 cm.
        How wide is the small rectangle?

9   Jason mixes 3 parts black paint with
    4 parts white paint to make dark grey
    paint.
    a)  How much white paint does he
        mix with 150 ml of black paint?
    b)  How much black paint does he mix
        with 1 litre of white paint?

10  In an election, the number of votes
    was shared between the Labour,
    Conservative and other parties in the
    ratio 5 : 4 : 2.
    Labour received 7500 votes.
    a)  How many votes did the
        Conservatives receive?
    b)  How many votes did the other
        parties receive?

# EXERCISE 9.4H

 Do not use your calculator for questions
1 to 5.

1   Share £40 between Paula and Tariq in
    the ratio 3 : 5.

2   Paint is mixed in the ratio 2 parts black
    paint to 3 parts white paint to make
    10 litres of grey paint.
    a)  How much black paint is used?
    b)  How much white paint is used?

3   A metal alloy is made up of copper, iron and nickel in the ratio 3 : 4 : 2. How much of each metal is there in 450 g of the alloy?

4   Inderjit worked 6 hours one day. The time he spent on filing, writing and computing was in the ratio 2 : 3 : 7. How long did he spend computing?

5   Daisy and Emily invested £5000 and £8000 respectively in a business venture. They agreed to share the profits in the ratio of their investment. Emily received £320. What was the total profit?

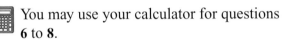 You may use your calculator for questions **6** to **8**.

6   Shahida spends her pocket money on sweets, magazines and clothes in the ratio 2 : 3 : 7. She receives £15 a week. How much does she spend on sweets?

7   In a questionnaire, the three possible answers are 'Yes', 'No' and 'Don't know'. The answers from a group of 456 people are in the ratio 10 : 6 : 3. How many 'Don't knows' are there?

8   Iain and Stephen bought a house between them in Spain. Iain paid 60% of the cost and Stephen 40%.
   a)   Write the ratio of the amounts they paid in its lowest terms.
   b)   The house cost 210 000 euros. How much did each pay?

# EXERCISE 9.5H

1   An 80 g bag of Munchoes costs 99p and a 200 g bag of Munchoes costs £2.19.
    Show which is better value.

2   Baxter's lemonade is sold in 2 litre bottles for £1.29 and in 3 litre bottles for £1.99.
    Show which is better value.

3   Butter is sold in 200 g tubs for 95p and in 450 g packets for £2.10.
    Show which is better value.

4   Fruit yoghurt is sold in packs of 4 tubs for 79p and in packs of 12 tubs for £2.19.
    Show which is better value.

5   There are two packs of minced meat on the reduced price shelf at the supermarket: a 1.8 kg pack reduced to £2.50 and a 1.5 kg pack reduced to £2.
    Show which is better value.

6   Smoothie shaving gel costs £1.19 for a 75 ml bottle and £2.89 for a 200 ml bottle.
    Show which is better value.

7   A supermarket sells cans of cola in two different sized packs: a pack of 12 cans costs £4.30 and a pack of 20 cans costs £7.25.
    Which pack is better value?

8   Sudso washing powder is sold in three sizes: 750 g for £3.15, 1.5 kg for £5.99 and 2.5 kg for £6.99.
    Which packet gives the best value?

##  EXERCISE 10.1H

Work these out mentally. As far as possible, write down only the final answer.

**1**
a)  8 + 25
b)  13 + 49
c)  0.6 + 5.2
d)  142 + 59
e)  187 + 25
f)  5.8 + 12.6
g)  326 + 9.3
h)  456 + 83
i)  1290 + 41
j)  8600 + 570

**2**
a)  12 − 5
b)  36 − 9
c)  10 − 0.4
d)  56 − 45
e)  82 − 39
f)  141 − 27
g)  1.2 − 0.7
h)  186 − 19
i)  307 − 81
j)  1200 − 153

**3**
a)  7 × 9
b)  12 × 8
c)  22 × 7
d)  11 × 12
e)  0.4 × 100
f)  19 × 7
g)  48 × 5
h)  25 × 8
i)  63 × 4
j)  42 × 21

**4**
a)  42 ÷ 7
b)  72 ÷ 12
c)  1500 ÷ 3
d)  184 ÷ 8
e)  240 ÷ 20
f)  108 ÷ 18
g)  96 ÷ 16
h)  16 ÷ 100
i)  24 ÷ 0.3
j)  3.6 ÷ 0.9

**5**
a)  7 + (−3)
b)  −2 + 6
c)  −5 + 7
d)  −4 + (−8)
e)  4 + (−9)
f)  −5 − 1
g)  6 − (−2)
h)  12 − (−8)
i)  −5 − (−10)
j)  −7 − (−3)

**6**
a)  12 × −2
b)  −4 × 5
c)  −6 × −3
d)  −10 × −4
e)  4 × −100
f)  10 ÷ −5
g)  −6 ÷ 2
h)  −20 ÷ −4
i)  −35 ÷ −5
j)  32 ÷ −4

**7** Write down the square of each of these numbers.
a)  7
b)  9
c)  12
d)  14
e)  1
f)  30
g)  200
h)  0.5
i)  0.8
j)  0.2

**8** Write down the square root of each of these numbers.
a)  36
b)  4
c)  64
d)  121
e)  144

**9** Write down the cube of each of these numbers.
a)  3
b)  4
c)  10
d)  50
e)  0.2

**10** A rectangle has sides 4.6 cm and 5.0 cm. Work out
a)  the perimeter of the rectangle.
b)  the area of the rectangle.

**11** Ayeesha spends £17.81. How much change does she get from £50?

**12** A square has area 121 cm². How long is its side?

13 Find 2% of £540.

14 Find two numbers which have a difference of 4 and whose product is 45.

15 Deepa has a 1 kg piece of cheese.
She eats 432 g of it.
How much is left?

# EXERCISE 10.2H

1 Round each of these numbers to 1 significant figure.
a) 14.3          b) 38
c) 6.54          d) 308
e) 1210          f) 0.78
g) 0.61          h) 0.053
i) 2413.5        j) 0.0097

2 Round each of these numbers to 1 significant figure.
a) 8.4           b) 18.36
c) 725           d) 8032
e) 98.3          f) 0.71
g) 0.0052        h) 0.019
i) 407.511       j) 23 095

3 Round each of these numbers to 2 significant figures.
a) 28.7          b) 149.3
c) 7832          d) 46 820
e) 21.36         f) 0.194
g) 0.0489        h) 0.003 61
i) 0.0508        j) 0.904

4 Round each of these numbers to 3 significant figures.
a) 7.385         b) 24.81
c) 28 462        d) 308.61
e) 16 418        f) 3.917
g) 60.72         h) 0.9135
i) 0.004 162     j) 2.236 06

For questions **5** to **12**, round the numbers in your calculations to 1 significant figure. Show your working.

5 Ashad bought 24 chocolate bars at 32p each. Estimate how much he spent.

6 Ramy earns £382 per week. Estimate his earnings in a year.

7 Mary drove 215 miles in 3 hours 48 minutes. Estimate her average speed.

8 A rectangle has length 9.2 cm and area 44.16 cm$^2$. Estimate its width.

9 A new computer is priced at £595 excluding VAT.
VAT at 17.5% must be paid on it. Estimate the amount of VAT to be paid.

10 A square paving slab has area 6000 cm$^2$. Estimate the length of a side of the slab.

11 A circle has radius 4.3 cm. Estimate its area.

12 Estimate the answers to these calculations.
a) $71 \times 58$          b) $\sqrt{46}$
c) $\dfrac{5987}{5.1}$     d) $19.1^2$
e) $62.7 \times 8316$      f) $\dfrac{5.72}{19.3}$
g) $\dfrac{32}{49.4}$      h) $8152 \times 37$
i) $\dfrac{935 \times 41}{8.5}$   j) $\dfrac{673 \times 0.76}{3.6 \times 2.38}$

# EXERCISE 10.3H

Give your answers to these questions as simply as possible.
Leave $\pi$ in your answers where appropriate.

1.  a) $2 \times 6 \times \pi$      b) $\pi \times 7^2$
    c) $\pi \times 12^2$      d) $2 \times 3.8 \times \pi$
    e) $\pi \times 11^2$

2.  a) $14\pi + 5\pi$
    b) $\pi \times 3^2 + \pi \times 6^2$
    c) $\pi \times 8^2 - \pi \times 4^2$
    d) $3 \times 42\pi$
    e) $\dfrac{36\pi}{4\pi}$

3.  Find the circumference of a circle with radius 15 cm.

4.  The areas of two circles are in the ratio $36\pi : 16\pi$. Simplify this ratio.

5.  A circular piece of card has radius 12 cm. A square piece is removed, with side 5 cm.
    Find the area that is left.

# EXERCISE 10.4H

1.  Work out these.
    a) $0.06 \times 600$      b) $0.03 \times 0.3$
    c) $0.9 \times 0.04$      d) $(0.05)^2$
    e) $(0.3)^2$      f) $500 \times 800$
    g) $30 \times 5000$      h) $5.1 \times 300$
    i) $20.3 \times 2000$  j) $1.82 \times 5000$

2.  Work out these.
    a) $300 \div 20$      b) $60 \div 2000$
    c) $3.6 \div 20$      d) $1.4 \div 0.2$
    e) $2.4 \div 3000$      f) $2.4 \div 0.03$
    g) $0.08 \div 0.004$  h) $5 \div 0.02$
    i) $400 \div 0.08$      j) $60 \div 0.15$

3.  Given that $4.5 \times 16.8 = 75.6$, work out these.
    a) $45 \times 1680$      b) $75.6 \div 168$
    c) $7560 \div 45$      d) $0.168 \times 0.045$
    e) $756 \div 0.168$

4.  Given that $702 \div 39 = 18$, work out these.
    a) $70\,200 \div 39$  b) $70.2 \div 3.9$
    c) $180 \times 39$      d) $7.02 \div 18$
    e) $1.8 \times 3.9$

5.  Given that $348 \times 216 = 75\,168$, work out these.
    a) $751\,680 \div 216$
    b) $34\,800 \times 2160$
    c) $3.48 \times 21.6$
    d) $751.68 \div 34.8$
    e) $0.348 \times 2160$

# 11 → ALGEBRA 1

## EXERCISE 11.1H

**1 a)** There are 6 men and 4 women on a bus. How many people are there on the bus?

**b)** There are 6 men and $w$ women on a bus.
Write an expression for the number of people on the bus.

**c)** There are $m$ men and $w$ women on a bus.
Write an expression for the number of people on the bus.

**2 a)** Shamsah buys 4 apples and 3 oranges.
How many pieces of fruit does she buy altogether?

**b)** Shamsah buys $x$ apples and 3 oranges.
Write an expression for the number of pieces of fruit she buys altogether.

**c)** Shamsah buys $x$ apples and $y$ oranges.
Write an expression for the number of pieces of fruit she buys altogether.

**3 a)** What is the length of this line?

$$\underline{\hspace{1cm}4\hspace{1cm}}\text{-----}\,{}^{7}\text{-----}$$

**b)** Write an expression for the length of this line.

$$\underline{\hspace{1cm}x\hspace{1cm}}\text{-----}\,{}^{7}\text{-----}$$

**c)** Write an expression for the length of this line.

$$\underline{\hspace{1cm}4\hspace{1cm}}\text{-----}\,{}^{x}\text{-----}$$

**4 a)** What is the length of this line?

$$\underline{\hspace{1cm}3\hspace{1cm}}\text{-----}\,{}^{5}\text{-----}$$

**b)** Write an expression for the length of this line.

$$\underline{\hspace{1cm}p\hspace{1cm}}\text{-----}\,{}^{5}\text{-----}$$

**c)** Write an expression for the length of this line.

$$\underline{\hspace{1cm}3\hspace{1cm}}\text{-----}\,{}^{q}\text{-----}$$

**5** Write an expression for the length of each of these lines.

**a)** $\underline{\hspace{1cm}x\hspace{1cm}}\text{-----}\,{}^{x}\text{-----}$

**b)** $\underline{\,{}^{2}\,}\text{-----}\,{}^{4}\text{-----}\underline{\hspace{0.5cm}x\hspace{0.5cm}}$

**c)** $\underline{\hspace{0.5cm}x\hspace{0.5cm}}\text{-----}\,{}^{4}\text{-----}\underline{\hspace{0.5cm}y\hspace{0.5cm}}$

**6** Write an expression for the length of each of these lines.

**a)** $\underline{\hspace{0.5cm}x\hspace{0.5cm}}\text{-----}\,{}^{y}\text{-----}\underline{\hspace{0.5cm}2\hspace{0.5cm}}$

**b)** $\underline{\hspace{0.5cm}x\hspace{0.5cm}}\text{-----}\,{}^{5}\text{-----}\underline{\hspace{0.5cm}x\hspace{0.5cm}}$

**c)** $\underline{\hspace{0.5cm}x\hspace{0.5cm}}\text{-----}\,{}^{y}\text{-----}\underline{\hspace{0.5cm}x\hspace{0.5cm}}$

**7** The length of a rectangle is 6 cm longer than its width.
  **a)** What is the length of the rectangle if the width is
    **(i)** 12 cm?    **(ii)** 16 cm?
  **b)** Write an expression for the length of the rectangle if the width is $w$ cm.

**8** There are $x$ people on a bus. At a bus stop, 5 more get on.
  Write an expression for the number of people now on the bus.

**9** Cox apples cost 10p more a kilogram than Braeburn apples.
  **a)** What is the cost of a kilogram of Cox apples when a kilogram of Braeburn apples costs
    **(i)** 85 pence?    **(ii)** 73 pence?
  **b)** Write an expression for the cost of a kilogram of Cox apples when a kilogram of Braeburn apples costs $x$ pence.

**10** At Pete's chip shop, chips cost $c$ pence a bag.
  Write an expression for the cost of
  **a)** 2 bags.  **b)** 4 bags.  **c)** 8 bags.

# EXERCISE 11.2H

**1** Pam has seven fewer books than James.
  **a)** How many books does Pam have if James has
    **(i)** 12 books?    **(ii)** 20 books?
  **b)** Write an expression for the number of books Pam has if James has $b$ books.

**2** Tea costs 20p a cup less than coffee.
  **a)** What is the cost of a cup of tea if a cup of coffee costs
    **(i)** 70p?    **(ii)** 95p?
  **b)** Write an expression for the cost of a cup of tea if a cup of coffee costs $c$ pence.

**3** Write expressions for the length of the dashed part of these lines.
  **a)**
  **b)**
  **c)**

**4** The width of a rectangle is 6 cm less than the length.
  **a)** What is the width of the rectangle if the length is
    **(i)** 12 cm?    **(ii)** 16 cm?
  **b)** Write an expression for the width of the rectangle if the length is $y$ cm.

**5** Mike earns £50 less per week than Adrian.
  **a)** How much does Mike earn per week if Adrian earns
    **(i)** £160?    **(ii)** £340?
  **b)** Write an expression for how much Mike earns per week if Adrian earns £$P$.

**6** There were 24 people on a bus when it arrived at a stop. Some got off.
  **a)** How many people were left on the bus if the number getting off was
    **(i)** 2?        **(ii)** 5?
  **b)** Write an expression for the number of people left on the bus if the number getting off was $s$.

**7** Joshua bought a coat that cost £$x$ less than the coat Jeremy bought.
  Write an expression for the cost of Joshua's coat if Jeremy's cost
  **a)** £65.        **b)** £80.        **c)** £$y$.

**8** The width of a rectangle is half its length.
  **a)** What is the width of the rectangle if the length is
    **(i)** 12 cm?        **(ii)** 16 cm?
  **b)** Write an expression for the width of the rectangle if the length is $y$ cm.

**9 a)** Write expressions for the length of the dashed part of these lines.
  **(i)**

  **(ii)**

  **b)** Write an expression for the length of this line.

**10** Joe spends £$x$ in $d$ days. He spends the same amount each day.
  Write an expression for the amount he spends in one day.

## EXERCISE 12.1H

Simplify these expressions.

1. $a + a + a$
2. $b + b + b + b + b + b + b + b$
3. $c \times 6$
4. $2 \times d$
5. $5 \times c + 2 \times c$
6. $c + c + c + c - c + c$
7. $2a + 3a - 2a$
8. $5 \times b$
9. $3c - 2c$
10. $4a + 3a$
11. $6x + 4x - 2x$
12. $7a - a$
13. $4y - 3y$
14. $2b + 4b - b$
15. $2p - 3p + 4p$
16. $6s + 2s - 3s - 4s$
17. $b + 2b$
18. $a + 2a - 3a$
19. $3 \times b + 4 \times b$
20. $5a + 2a$

## EXERCISE 12.2H

Simplify these expressions where possible.

1. $4a + 2b + a + b$
2. $3a + 2b - 2a$
3. $5 \times c \times d$
4. $5c + 3d$
5. $a + 2b + 4a + b$
6. $2 \times p + 3 \times q$
7. $3 \times a \times 4 \times b$
8. $2x + 4y + y + 2x$
9. $5 \times a \times a$
10. $6a + b + 3c + b + 3a + 3c$
11. $4a + 2a - 3a + a$
12. $2 \times a \times b + 4a \times a$
13. $3a - 2b$
14. $b \times b$
15. $4s + 2 - 3s + 3$
16. $a + 2b - a + 2b$
17. $2 \times a \times b \times b$
18. $3x + 2y + 4 + 2y - 2x + 3$
19. $a + 2b + 2a - 3b$
20. $2a \times 2b \times 3a \times b$

# 13 → ALGEBRA 3

## EXERCISE 13.1H

Expand these.

1 $7(3a + 6b)$      2 $5(2c + 3d)$
3 $4(3e - 5f)$      4 $3(7g - 2h)$
5 $3(4i + 2j - 3k)$    6 $3(5m - 2n + 3p)$
7 $6(4r - 3s - 2t)$    8 $8(4r + 2s + t)$
9 $4(3u + 5v)$      10 $6(4w + 3x)$
11 $2(5y + z)$      12 $4(3y + 2z)$
13 $5(3v + 2)$      14 $3(7 + 4w)$
15 $5(1 - 3a)$      16 $3(8g - 5)$

## EXERCISE 13.2H

Expand the brackets and simplify these.

1   a) $3(4a + 5) + 2(3a + 4)$
    b) $5(4b + 3) + 3(2b + 1)$
    c) $2(3 + 6c) + 4(5 + 7c)$

2   a) $2(4x + 5) + 3(5x - 2)$
    b) $4(3y + 2) + 5(3y - 2)$
    c) $3(4 + 7z) + 2(3 - 5z)$

3   a) $4(4s + 3t) + 5(2s + 3t)$
    b) $3(4v + 5w) + 2(3v + 2w)$
    c) $6(2x + 5y) + 3(4x + 2y)$
    d) $2(5v + 4w) + 3(2v + w)$

4   a) $5(2n + 5p) + 4(2n - 5p)$
    b) $3(4q + 6r) + 5(2q - 3r)$
    c) $7(3d + 2e) + 5(3d - 2e)$
    d) $5(3f + 8g) + 4(3f - 9g)$
    e) $4(5h - 6j) - 6(2h - 5j)$
    f) $4(5k - 6m) - 3(2k - 5m)$

## EXERCISE 13.3H

Factorise these as fully as possible.

1   a) $8x + 20$     b) $3x + 6$
    c) $9x - 12$     d) $5x - 30$

2   a) $16 + 8x$     b) $9 + 15x$
    c) $12 - 16x$     d) $8 - 12x$

3   a) $4x^2 + 16x$     b) $6x^2 + 30x$
    c) $8x^2 - 20x$     d) $9x^2 - 15x$

## EXERCISE 13.4H

Expand the brackets and simplify these.

1   a) $(a + 5)(a + 3)$
    b) $(b + 2)(b + 4)$
    c) $(4 + c)(3 + c)$

2   a) $(2d + 3)(4d - 3)$
    b) $(5e + 4)(3e - 2)$
    c) $(3 + 8f)(2 - 5f)$

3   a) $(3g - 2)(5g - 6)$
    b) $(4h - 5)(3h - 7)$
    c) $(5j - 6)(3j - 8)$

4   a) $(3k + 7)(4k - 5)$
    b) $(2 + 7m)(3 - 8m)$
    c) $(4 + 3n)(2 - 5n)$

5   a) $(2 + 5p)(3 - 7p)$
    b) $(5r - 6)(2r - 5)$
    c) $(3s - 2)(4s - 9)$

# EXERCISE 13.5H

Simplify each of the following, writing your answer using index notation.

1  a) $7 \times 7 \times 7 \times 7 \times 7$
   b) $3 \times 3 \times 3 \times 3 \times 3$
   c) $2 \times 2 \times 2 \times 2 \times 2 \times 2$

2  a) $d \times d \times d \times d \times d \times d \times d$
   b) $m \times m \times m \times m \times m \times m$
   c) $t \times t \times t \times t \times t \times t \times t$

3  a) $a \times a \times a \times a \times b \times b$
   b) $c \times c \times c \times c \times d \times d \times d \times d \times d$
   c) $r \times r \times r \times s \times s \times t \times t \times t \times t$

4  a) $2x \times 3y \times 6z$
   b) $2a \times 3b \times 4c$
   c) $r \times 2s \times 3t \times 4s \times 5r$

# 14 → FORMULAE 1

## EXERCISE 14.1H

1   The total number of seats in an assembly hall is found by multiplying the number of rows by 20.
    How many seats are there when there are
    a) 20 rows?        b) 15 rows?
    c) 17 rows?        d) $13\frac{1}{2}$ rows?

2   The perimeter of a square is found by multiplying the length of one side by 4.
    Work out the perimeter of a square with sides of these lengths.
    a) 5 cm            b) 13 cm
    c) $6\frac{1}{2}$ cm         d) 8.2 cm

3   The cost of a child's bus fare is half the cost of an adult's fare. What is the cost of a child's fare when the adult fare is
    a) 80p?            b) 70p?
    c) £1.30?          d) £2.36?

4   Five friends divide a bag of sweets equally. To work out how many sweets each person receives, divide the total number of sweets by 5.
    How many sweets does each person receive when the bag contains
    a) 20 sweets?      b) 55 sweets?
    c) 80 sweets?      d) 125 sweets?

5   The time, in minutes, needed to cook a piece of beef can be found by multiplying the weight of the beef in kilograms by 40. How long does it take to cook a piece of beef weighing
    a) 2 kg?           b) 8 kg?
    c) $5\frac{1}{2}$ kg?       d) 3.2 kg?

6   The area of a rectangular room is found by multiplying the length by the width. Work out the area of these rooms.
    a) Length 4 m and width 3 m
    b) Length and width both 7 m
    c) Length $2\frac{1}{2}$ m and width 6 m
    d) Length 5.4 m and width 5 m

7   A car hire firm charges a fee of £30, plus £2 for each mile travelled.
    How much is the total charge if you travel
    a) 25 miles?       b) 70 miles?
    c) 400 miles?      d) 185 miles?

8   A football team earns 3 points for every match they win and 1 point for every match they draw. How many points in total do they earn when they
    a) win 3 games and draw 5?
    b) win 7 games and draw 10?
    c) win 14 games and draw 6?
    d) win 28 games and draw 3?

9 To change American dollars into pounds, divide the number of dollars by 1.5.
How many pounds you will get for
a)  $6?          b)  $150?
c)  $24?          d)  $10.50?

10 To change a distance from miles into kilometres, multiply the number of miles by 8 and divide by 5.
Work out the number of kilometres that is the same as
a)  10 miles.          b)  15 miles.
c)  100 miles.          d)  44 miles.

# EXERCISE 14.2H

In questions **1** to **7**, write down a formula for each situation using the letters in **bold**.

1  The total number of **s**eats in an assembly hall is found by multiplying the number of **r**ows by 20.

2  The **p**erimeter of a square is found by multiplying the **l**ength of one side by 4.

3  The cost of a **c**hild's bus fare is half the cost of an **a**dult's fare.

4  Five friends divide a bag of sweets equally.
To work out how many sweets **e**ach person receives, divide the total number of **s**weets by 5.

5  The **t**ime, in minutes, needed to cook a piece of beef can be found by multiplying the **w**eight of the beef in kilograms by 40.

6  The **a**rea of a rectangular room is found by multiplying the **l**ength by the **w**idth.

7  A car hire firm **c**harges a fee of £30, plus £2 for each **m**ile travelled.

In questions **8** to **10**, write down a formula for the situation using appropriate letters and say what each letter stands for.

8  A football team earns 3 points for every match they win and 1 point for every match they draw.

9  To change American dollars into pounds, divide the number of dollars by 1.5.

10 To change a distance from miles into kilometres, multiply the number of miles by 8 and divide by 5.

# EXERCISE 14.3H

1  Find the value of these expressions when $a = 4$ and $b = 2$.
a)  $a + b$               b)  $a - b$
c)  $2a$                  d)  $7a$
e)  $5b$                  f)  $8b$
g)  $ab$                  h)  $a^2$
i)  $3ab$                 j)  $2a + b$
k)  $3a - b$              l)  $5a + 4b$
m) $3a - 4b$              n)  $a^2 + b^2$
o)  $3a^2$                p)  $6b^2$
q)  $a^2b$                r)  $b^3$
s)  $\dfrac{a}{b}$        t)  $\dfrac{10b}{a}$
u)  $b - a$               v)  $\dfrac{4b}{2a}$
w)  $\dfrac{a^2}{b^2}$    x)  $\dfrac{b}{a}$

2  Use the formula $C = 5t + 2$ to find $C$ when $t$ has the following values.
a)  $t = 2$     b)  $t = 8$     c)  $t = 12$
d)  $t = 20$    e)  $t = \frac{1}{2}$

3   Use the formula $P = 2C - F$ to find $P$
    when $C$ and $F$ have the following values.
    a)  $C = 4, F = 4$
    b)  $C = 3, F = 5$
    c)  $C = 8, F = 5$
    d)  $C = 0, F = 7$

4   Use the formula $X = w + nd$ to find $X$
    when $w$, $n$ and $d$ have the following
    values.
    a)  $w = 1, n = 2, d = 1$
    b)  $w = 4, n = 2, d = 6$
    c)  $w = 12, n = 10, d = 0$
    d)  $w = 50, n = 30, d = 10$
    e)  $w = 11, n = 9, d = \frac{1}{2}$

5   Find the value of these expressions
    when $k = 3$ and $m = 2$.
    a)  $k + m$      b)  $5k$      c)  $km$
    d)  $m - k$      e)  $4k + 6m$

# REVIEW EXERCISE 14H

1   Use the formula:
    **total cost = number of
    days worked** $\times$ £2000 + £500
    Find the **total cost** when the **number
    of days worked** = 6.

2   The following formula is used to
    calculate the cost of repairing a gas
    boiler:
    **cost = rate per hour** $\times$ **number
    of hours + standing charge**
    a)  Calculate the **cost** when:
        **rate per hour** = £4.00
        **number of hours** = 5
        **standing charge** = £25.00

    b)  Calculate the **standing charge**
        when:
        **cost** = £50.00
        **rate per hour** = £6.00
        **number of hours** = 3

3   The cost, in pounds, of hiring a van is
    given by the following formula:
    **cost = number of hours** $\times$ 5 + 20
    a)  Find the **cost** of hiring a van for
        6 hours.
    b)  Tim paid £85. Find the **number of
        hours** for which Tim hired the van.

4   The cost, in pounds, of hiring a cement
    mixer is given by the formula:
    **cost = number of hours** $\times$ 7 + 20
    a)  Find the **cost** when the cement
        mixer is hired for 12 hours.
    b)  Find the **number of hours** a
        cement mixer is hired for when the
        cost is £125.

5   The formula shown below is used to
    calculate the amount paid, in pounds,
    to repair a television set.
    **amount paid** = 12.25 $\times$ **number
    of hours** + 55
    a)  Calculate the **amount paid** when
        the number of hours is 13.
    b)  Calculate the **number of hours**
        when the amount paid is
        153 pounds.

## EXERCISE 15.1H

1   Pearl is a child minder. She charges
    £3.50 an hour.
    She looks after Mrs Khan's child for
    6 hours. How much does she charge?

2   It costs £60 plus £1 a mile to hire a
    coach.
    a)  How much does it cost to hire a
        coach to go
        (i)   80 miles?
        (ii)  150 miles?
    b)  Write a formula for the cost, £C, of
        hiring a coach to go n miles.

3   The cost of booking a room for a
    meeting is £80 plus £20 an hour.
    a)  How much does it cost to hire the
        room for
        (i)   5 hours?
        (ii)  8 hours?
    b)  Write a formula for the cost, £C, of
        hiring the room for h hours.

4   The perimeter of a rectangle is twice
    the length plus twice the width.
    a)  What is the perimeter of a
        rectangle with length 5 cm and
        width 3.5 cm?
    b)  Write a formula for the perimeter,
        P, of a rectangle with length x and
        width y.

5   To find the volume of a pyramid,
    multiply the area of the base by the
    height and divide by 3.
    a)  What is the volume of a pyramid
        with base area 12 cm$^2$ and height
        7 cm?
    b)  Write a formula for the volume, V,
        of a pyramid with base area A and
        height h.

6   To find the time it takes to type a
    document, divide the number of words
    in the document by the number of
    words typed per minute.
    a)  How long does it take Liz to type a
        document 560 words long if she
        types 80 words a minute?
    b)  Write a formula for the time, T, to
        type a document w words long if
        the typist types r words a minute.

7   The time, t, for a journey is the
    distance, d, divided by the speed, s.
    a)  Write a formula for this.
    b)  Steve travelled 175 miles at a
        speed of 50 mph. How long did the
        journey take?

8   The circumference of a circle is given
    by the formula:
    $C = \pi \times D$, where D is the
    diameter of the circle.

    Find the circumference of a circle with
    diameter 8.5 cm. Use $\pi = 3.14$.

**9** At Carterknowle toddlers group, the charge is £1 per carer and 50p for every toddler they bring.
  **a)** Tracey brings three toddlers to the group.
  How much does she pay?
  **b)** Fran brings $n$ toddlers to the group. Write down an equation for the amount, $£A$, she has to pay.

**10 a)** For the formula $A = b - c$, find $A$ when $b = 6$ and $c = 3.5$.
  **b)** For the formula $B = 2a - b$, find $B$ when $a = 6$ and $b = 5$.
  **c)** For the formula $C = 2a - b + 3c$, find $C$ when $a = 3.5$, $b = 2.6$ and $c = 1.2$.
  **d)** For the formula $D = 3b^2$, find $D$ when $b = 2$.
  **e)** For the formula $E = ab - cd$, find $E$ when $a = 12.5$, $b = 6$, $c = 3.5$ and $d = 8$.
  **f)** For the formula $F = \dfrac{a - b}{5}$, find $F$ when $a = 6$ and $b = 3.5$.

# EXERCISE 15.2H

**1** Rearrange each of these formulae to make the letter in brackets the subject.
  **a)** $a = b + c$  $(b)$
  **b)** $a = 3x - y$  $(x)$
  **c)** $a = b + ct$  $(t)$
  **d)** $F = 2(q + p)$  $(q)$
  **e)** $x = 2y - 3z$  $(y)$
  **f)** $P = \dfrac{3 + 4n}{5}$  $(n)$

**2** The formula for the circumference of a circle is $C = \pi d$.
Rearrange the formula to make $d$ the subject.

**3** Rearrange the formula $A = \dfrac{3ab}{2n}$ to make
  **a)** $a$ the subject.
  **b)** $n$ the subject.

**4** The formula for finding the perimeter of a rectangle is $P = 2(a + b)$, where $P$ is the perimeter, $a$ is the length of the rectangle and $b$ is the width of the rectangle.
Rearrange the formula to make $a$ the subject.

**5** The formula $y = mx + c$ is the equation of a straight line.
Rearrange it to find $m$ in terms of $x$, $y$ and $c$.

**6** The surface area of a sphere is given by the formula $A = 4\pi r^2$.
Rearrange the formula to make $r$ the subject.

**7** The formula for the volume of this prism is $V = \dfrac{\pi r^2 h}{4}$.

  **a)** Find $V$ when $r = 2.5$ and $h = 7$.
  **b) (i)** Rearrange the formula to make $r$ the subject.
    **(ii)** Find $r$ when $V = 100$ and $h = 10$.

**8** The formula for the surface area of a closed cylinder is $S = 2\pi r(r + h)$.
Rearrange the formula to make $h$ the subject.

# 16 → SEQUENCES 1

## EXERCISE 16.1H

1   Find the first four terms of each of these sequences.
    a)  First term 3, term-to-term rule Add 5
    b)  First term −5, term-to-term rule Add 2
    c)  First term 23, term-to-term rule Subtract 5
    d)  First term 60, term-to-term rule Subtract 25
    e)  First term −17, term-to-term rule Add 6
    f)  First term −1, term-to-term rule Add $\frac{1}{2}$

2   Write down the next two terms in each of these sequences and give the term-to-term rule.
    a)  1, 8, 15, 22, 29, 36, ...
    b)  7, 13, 19, 25, 31, 37, ...
    c)  9, 17, 25, 33, 41, 49, ...
    d)  4, 13, 22, 31, 40, 49, ...
    e)  16, 21, 26, 31, 36, 41, ...
    f)  23, 30, 37, 44, 51, 58, ...

3   Write down the next two terms in each of these sequences and give the term-to-term rule.
    a)  41, 35, 29, 23, 17, 11, ...
    b)  39, 32, 25, 18, 11, 4, ...
    c)  26, 21, 16, 11, 6, 1, ...
    d)  29, 23, 17, 11, 5, −1, ...
    e)  43, 35, 27, 19, 11, 3, ...
    f)  68, 55, 42, 29, 16, 3, ...

4   Find the missing numbers in each of these sequences and give the term-to-term rule.
    a)  1, 7, ..., 19, 25, ...
    b)  11, ..., 35, 47, ..., 71
    c)  85, ..., 67, ..., 49, 40
    d)  ..., 87, 83, 79, ..., 71
    e)  7, 22, ..., ..., 67, 82
    f)  34, ..., 20, 13, 6, ...

## EXERCISE 16.2H

1   Draw the next diagram in each of these sequences.
    For each sequence, count the dots in each diagram and find the term-to-term rule.

    a)

    b) ![dots]

    c) ![dots]

    d) ![dots]

**2** Draw the next diagram in each of these sequences.
For each sequence, count the lines in each diagram and find the term-to-term rule.

a)

b)

c)

d)

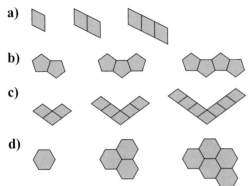

# EXERCISE 16.3H

**1** **a)** Write down the next term of the sequence

   3   8   13   18   23   ...

   **b)** Write down, in words, the rule for continuing the following sequence

   88   79   70   61   52   ...

**2** **a)** Write down the next term in the sequence

   4   8   12   16   20   ...

   **b)** Dots are used to make a sequence of patterns. The first three patterns are shown below.

   Draw the fourth pattern.

**3** **a)** Write down the next two terms in the sequence

   4   11   18   25   32   ...   ...

   **b)** Triangles, ▽, are used to make a sequence of patterns.
   The first three patterns are shown below.

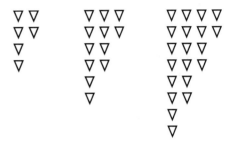

   Draw the fourth pattern.

**4** Write down the next two numbers in the sequence

   27   25   21   15   ...   ...

**5** Write down the first three terms of the sequence whose $n$th term is $n^2 - 2$.

**6** **a)** Write down the next term in the following sequence

   5   8   12   17   ...

   **b)** Dots are used to draw a sequence of patterns. The first three patterns are shown below.

   Draw the next shape in the pattern.

7 Dots are used to make a sequence of patterns.
The first three patterns are shown below.

```
                        •
         •   •    • •
  •      • •      • • •
```

Draw the **fifth** shape.

8   96    48    24    12    6    …

    **a)** Write down the next term in the above sequence.

    **b)** Describe, in words, the rule for finding the next term of the above sequence.

# 17 → SEQUENCES 2

## EXERCISE 17.1H

1   Look at this sequence of circles.
    The first four patterns in the sequence
    have been drawn.

    ○        ○ ○        ○ ○ ○
    ○        ○ ○        ○ ○ ○        ○ ○ ○
                                     ○ ○ ○ ○

    a)  How many circles are there in the
        100th pattern?
    b)  Describe the position-to-term rule
        for this sequence.

2   Look at this sequence of matchstick
    patterns.

    a)  Copy and complete this table.

    | Pattern number | 1 | 2 | 3 | 4 | 5 |
    |---|---|---|---|---|---|
    | Number of matchsticks | | | | | |

    b)  What patterns can you see in the
        numbers?
    c)  Find the number of matchsticks in
        the 50th pattern.

3   Here is a sequence of star patterns.

                                    *   *   *
                    *   *       *   *   *
        *           *   *       *   *   *
        *           *   *       *   *   *

    a)  Draw the next pattern in the
        sequence.
    b)  Without drawing the pattern, find the
        number of stars in the 8th pattern.
        Explain how you found your answer.

4   The numbers in a sequence are given
    by the rule multiply the position
    number by 7, then subtract 10.

    a)  Show that the first term of the
        sequence is $-3$.
    b)  Find the next four terms in the
        sequence.

5   Find the first four terms of the
    sequences with these $n$th terms.
    a)  $10n$          b)  $8n + 2$

6   Find the first five terms of the
    sequences with these $n$th terms.
    a)  $n^2$          b)  $2n^2$          c)  $5n^2$

7   The first term of a sequence is 3.
    The general rule for the sequence is
    multiply a term by 3 to get to the next
    term.
    Write down the first five terms of the
    sequence.

**8** For a sequence, $T_1 = 12$ and
$T_{n+1} = T_n - 5$.
Write down the first four terms of this sequence.

**9** Draw suitable patterns to represent this sequence.

$$1, 4, 7, 10, \ldots$$

**10** Draw suitable patterns to represent this sequence.

$$1 \times 1, 3 \times 3, 5 \times 5, 7 \times 7, \ldots$$

# EXERCISE 17.2H

**1** Find the $n$th term for each of these sequences.
a) $10, 13, 16, 19, 22, \ldots$
b) $0, 1, 2, 3, 4, \ldots$
c) $-3, -1, 1, 3, 5, \ldots$

**2** Find the $n$th term for each of these sequences.
a) $25, 20, 15, 10, 5, \ldots$
b) $4, 2, 0, -2, -4, \ldots$
c) $3, 2, 1, 0, -1, \ldots$

**3** Which of these sequences are linear?
Find the next two terms of each of the sequences that are linear.
a) $2, 5, 10, 17, \ldots$
b) $2, 5, 8, 11, \ldots$
c) $1, 3, 6, 10, \ldots$
d) $12, 8, 4, 0, -4, \ldots$

**4** a) Write down the first five terms of the sequence with $n$th term $100n$.
b) Compare your answers with this sequence.
$$99, 199, 299, 399, \ldots$$
Write down the $n$th term of this sequence.

**5** A mail-order shirt company charges £25 per shirt, plus an overall delivery charge of £3.
a) Copy and complete the table.

| Number of shirts | 1 | 2 | 3 |
|---|---|---|---|
| Cost in £ | | | |

b) Write an expression for the cost, in pounds, of $n$ shirts.
c) Paul pays £128 for shirts. How many does he buy?

**6** a) Write down the first five terms of the sequence with $n$th term $n^2$.
b) Compare your answers with this sequence.
$$0, 3, 8, 15, 24, \ldots$$
Write the $n$th term of this sequence.

**7** The $n$th triangle number is $\dfrac{n(n+1)}{2}$.
Find the 60th triangle number.

**8** The $n$th term of a sequence is $2^n$.
a) Write down the first five terms of this sequence.
b) Describe the sequence.

**9** a) Write down the first five cube numbers.
b) Compare the sequence below with the sequence of cube numbers.
$$3, 10, 29, 66, 127, \ldots$$
Use what you notice to write down the $n$th term of this sequence.
c) Find the 10th term of this sequence.

**10** Find the $n$th term of each of the following sequences.
a) $1 \times 2, 2 \times 3, 3 \times 4, 4 \times 5, \ldots$
b) $1 \times 3, 2 \times 5, 3 \times 7, 4 \times 9, \ldots$
c) $2 \times 1, 4 \times 3, 6 \times 5, 8 \times 7, \ldots$

# 18 → COORDINATES

## EXERCISE 18.1H

1   Write down the coordinates of the points A, B, C, D, E, F, G, H, I and J.

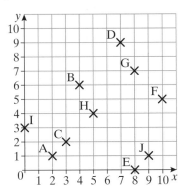

2   On a grid, draw x- and y-axes from 0 to 8. Plot and label these points.
A(7, 1)      B(3, 5)      C(4, 2)
D(2, 0)      E(0, 6)

## EXERCISE 18.2H

1   Write down the coordinates of the points A, B, C, D, E, F, G, H, I and J.

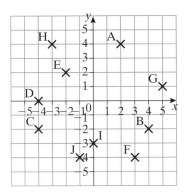

In questions **2** to **9** you will need to draw x- and y-axes from −5 to +5.

2   Plot and label the points A(5, 1), B(5, −3), C(−3, −3) and D(−3, 1). Join the points to make the shape ABCD. What is the special name of the shape ABCD?

3   Plot and label the points A(4, 1), B(4, −4) and C(−3, −4). Join the points to make the shape ABC. What is the special name of the shape ABC?

4   Plot and label the points A(2, 4), B(2, −2), C(−1, −4) and D(−1, 2). Join the points to make the shape ABCD. What is the special name of the shape ABCD?

5   Plot and label the points A(2, 2), B(5, −3), C(−1, −3) and D(−2, 2). Join the points to make the shape ABCD. What is the special name of the shape ABCD?

6   Plot and label the points A(1, 3), B(1, −4) and C(−3, −4). Mark the point D so that ABCD is a rectangle. Write down the coordinates of D.

7   Plot and label the points A(1, 1), B(5, −1) and D(−3, −1). Mark the point C so that ABCD is a rhombus. Write down the coordinates of C.

8   Plot and label the points A(−1, 4), B(1, 0) and C(−3, −2). Mark the point D so that ABCD is a square. Write down the coordinates of D.

**9** Plot and label the points A(−2, 2), B(3, 3) and C(1, −2). Mark the point D so that ABCD is a parallelogram. Write down the coordinates of D.

## EXERCISE 18.3H

**1** Write down the equation of each of the lines **a)**, **b)**, **c)** and **d)**.

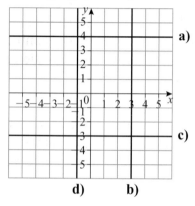

d)          b)

For questions **2** to **4** use a single grid with axes labelled from −7 to 7.

**2** Copy and complete this table of values for the equation $y = x + 2$.

| x | −3 | −2 | −1 | 0 | 1 | 2 | 3 |
|---|----|----|----|---|---|---|---|
| y | −1 |    | 1  |   | 3 |   |   |

Plot the points on your grid and join them with a straight line.

**3** Copy and complete this table of values for the equation $y = x - 4$.

| x | −3 | −2 | −1 | 0 | 1 | 2 | 3 | 4 | 5 |
|---|----|----|----|---|---|---|---|---|---|
| y | −7 |    | −5 |   | −3 |   | −1 |   |   |

Plot the points on your grid and join them with a straight line.

**4** Copy and complete this table of values for the equation $x + y = 5$.

| x | −1 | 0 | 1 | 2 | 3 | 4 | 5 | 6 |
|---|----|---|---|---|---|---|---|---|
| y | 6  |   | 4 |   | 2 |   | 0 |   |

Plot the points on your grid and join them with a straight line.

**5** What are the coordinates of the point where the lines in questions **3** and **4** cross?

For questions **6** and **7** use a single grid with axes labelled from −8 to 8.

**6** Copy and complete this table of values for the equation $y = 2x - 3$.

| x | −2 | −1 | 0 | 1 | 2 | 3 | 4 | 5 |
|-----|----|----|---|----|---|---|---|---|
| 2x  |    | −2 |   | 2  |   |   | 8 |   |
| −3  |    | −3 |   | −3 |   |   | −3 |   |
| y   |    | −5 |   | −1 |   |   | 5 |   |

Plot the points on your grid and join them with a straight line.

**7** Copy and complete this table of values for the equation $y = 6 - x$.
Remember: $6 - (-2) = 6 + 2 = 8$.

| x | −2 | −1 | 0 | 1 | 2 | 3 | 4 | 5 | 6 | 7 |
|---|----|----|---|---|---|---|---|---|---|---|
| y | 8  |    |   | 5 |   |   | 2 |   | 0 |   |

Plot the points on your grid and join them with a straight line.

**8** What are the coordinates of the point where the lines in questions **6** and **7** cross?

## EXERCISE 19.1H

Solve these equations.

1 $x - 5 = 12$    2 $5x = 40$

3 $9y = 45$    4 $x + 7 = 18$

5 $10p = 60$    6 $2x = 2$

7 $3x = 18$    8 $6y = 48$

9 $x - 2 = -5$    10 $x - 12 = -4$

11 $x - 10 = -2$    12 $x - 11 = -11$

## EXERCISE 19.2H

Solve these equations.

1 $15 - x = 9$    2 $7 - x = 10$

3 $3x + 2 = 11$    4 $4x + 1 = 17$

5 $3x - 5 = 7$    6 $3x + 6 = 48$

7 $3x - 7 = 41$    8 $8x - 3 = 29$

9 $4x + 12 = 20$    10 $4x + 18 = 22$

11 $5x + 6 = 31$    12 $2x - 4 = -2$

## EXERCISE 19.3H

Solve these equations.

1 $\dfrac{x}{4} = 7$    2 $\dfrac{a}{3} = 6$    3 $\dfrac{p}{7} = 7$

4 $\dfrac{y}{4} = 12$    5 $\dfrac{x}{2} = 18$    6 $\dfrac{x}{4} = 6$

7 $\dfrac{x}{3} = 7$    8 $\dfrac{x}{5} = 5$    9 $\dfrac{x}{6} = 1$

10 $\dfrac{x}{3} = 3$    11 $\dfrac{x}{3} = 9$    12 $\dfrac{x}{4} = 20$

## EXERCISE 19.4H

1   Robbie thinks of a number.
    He adds 3 to it. The answer is 8.
    Use $x$ to represent Robbie's number.
    Write down and solve an equation to
    find Robbie's number.

2   Patsy thinks of a number.
    She multiplies it by 3. The answer is 15.
    Use $x$ to represent Patsy's number.
    Write down and solve an equation to
    find Patsy's number.

3   Four chocolate biscuits cost 64p.
    Use $c$ to represent the cost of one
    biscuit in pence.
    Write down and solve an equation to
    find the cost of one biscuit.

4   Patel has 16 CDs. Sonia has $x$ CDs.
    Together they have 34 CDs.
    Write down and solve an equation to
    find how many CDs Sonia has.

5   Joy had $x$ pens.
    She gives away 6 of them and has 7 left.
    Write down and solve an equation
    to find how many pens Joy had to
    start with.

# 20 → EQUATIONS AND INEQUALITIES

## EXERCISE 20.1H

Solve these equations.

1. $2x - 3 = 7$
2. $2x + 2 = 8$
3. $2x - 9 = 3$
4. $3x - 2 = 7$
5. $6x + 2 = 26$
6. $3x + 2 = 17$
7. $4x - 5 = 3$
8. $4x + 2 = 8$
9. $2x - 7 = 10$
10. $5x + 12 = 7$
11. $x^2 + 3 = 19$
12. $x^2 - 2 = 7$
13. $y^2 - 1 = 80$
14. $11 - 3x = 2$
15. $4x - 12 = -18$

## EXERCISE 20.2H

Solve these equations.

1. $3(x - 2) = 18$
2. $2(1 + x) = 8$
3. $3(x - 5) = 6$
4. $2(x + 3) = 10$
5. $5(x - 2) = 15$
6. $2(x + 3) = 10$

7. $5(x - 4) = 20$
8. $4(x + 1) = 16$
9. $2(x - 7) = 8$
10. $3(2x + 3) = 18$
11. $5(2x - 3) = 15$
12. $2(3x - 2) = 14$
13. $5(2x - 3) = 40$
14. $4(x - 3) = 6$
15. $2(2x - 3) = 8$

## EXERCISE 20.3H

Solve these equations.

1. $5x - 1 = 3x + 5$
2. $5x + 1 = 2x + 13$
3. $7x - 2 = 2x + 8$
4. $6x + 1 = 4x + 21$
5. $9x - 10 = 4x + 5$
6. $5x - 8 = 3x - 6$
7. $6x + 2 = 10 - 2x$
8. $2x - 10 = 5 - 3x$
9. $15 + 3x = 2x + 18$
10. $2x - 5 = 4 - x$
11. $3x - 2 = x + 7$
12. $x - 1 = 2x - 6$
13. $2x - 4 = 2 - x$
14. $9 - x = x + 5$
15. $3x - 2 = x - 8$

# EXERCISE 20.4H

Solve these equations.

**1** $\dfrac{x}{2} = 7$

**2** $\dfrac{x}{5} - 2 = 1$

**3** $\dfrac{x}{4} + 5 = 8$

**4** $\dfrac{x}{3} - 5 = 5$

**5** $\dfrac{x}{6} + 3 = 4$

**6** $\dfrac{x}{5} + 1 = 4$

**7** $\dfrac{x}{8} - 3 = 9$

**8** $\dfrac{x}{4} + 1 = 3$

**9** $\dfrac{x}{7} + 5 = 6$

**10** $\dfrac{x}{4} + 5 = 4$

# EXERCISE 20.5H

**1** Calculate the value of $x^3 + x$ when
   **a)** $x = 2$.
   **b)** $x = 3$.
   **c)** $x = 2.5$.

**2 a)** Calculate the value of $x^3 - x$ when
   **(i)** $x = 4$.    **(ii)** $x = 5$.
   **(iii)** $x = 4.6$.    **(iv)** $x = 4.7$.
   **(v)** $x = 4.65$.
   **b)** Using your answers to part **a)**, give the solution of $x^3 - x = 94$, to 1 decimal place.

Use trial and improvement for questions **3** to **10**. Show your trials.

**3** Find a solution, between $x = 2$ and $x = 3$, to the equation $x^3 = 11$. Give your answer correct to 1 decimal place.

**4 a)** Show that a solution to the equation $x^3 + 3x = 30$ lies between $x = 2$ and $x = 3$.
   **b)** Find the solution correct to 1 decimal place.

**5 a)** Show that a solution to the equation $x^3 - 2x = 70$ lies between $x = 4$ and $x = 5$.
   **b)** Find the solution correct to 1 decimal place.

**6** Find a solution to the equation $x^3 + 4x = 100$. Give your answer correct to 1 decimal place.

**7** Find a solution to the equation $x^3 + x = 60$. Give your answer correct to 2 decimal places.

**8** Find a solution to the equation $x^3 - x^2 = 40$. Give your answer correct to 2 decimal places.

**9** A number, $x$, added to the square of that number, is equal to 1000.
   **a)** Write this as a formula.
   **b)** Find the number correct to 1 decimal place.

**10** The cube of a number minus the number is equal to 600.
   Find the number correct to 2 decimal places.

# EXERCISE 20.6H

For each of questions **1** to **5**, solve the inequality and show the solution on a number line.

1  $x - 2 > 1$

2  $x + 1 < 3$

3  $3x - 2 \geqslant 7$

4  $2x + 1 \leqslant 6$

5  $3x - 6 \geqslant 0$

For each of questions **6** to **15**, solve the inequality.

6  $7 \leqslant 2x - 1$

7  $5x < x + 12$

8  $4x \geqslant x + 9$

9  $4 + x < 0$

10  $3x + 1 \leqslant 2x + 6$

11  $2(x - 3) > x$

12  $5(x + 1) > 3x + 10$

13  $7x + 5 \leqslant 2x + 30$

14  $5x + 2 < 7x - 4$

15  $3(3x + 2) \geqslant 2(x + 10)$

**20 Equations and inequalities**

## EXERCISE 21.1H

**1** Draw the graph of $y = 3x$ for values of $x$ from $-3$ to 3.

**2** Draw the graph of $y = x + 2$ for values of $x$ from $-4$ to 2.

**3** Draw the graph of $y = 4x + 2$ for values of $x$ from $-3$ to 3.

**4** Draw the graph of $y = 2x - 5$ for values of $x$ from $-1$ to 5.

**5** Draw the graph of $y = -2x - 4$ for values of $x$ from $-4$ to 2.

## EXERCISE 21.2H

**1** Draw the graph of $3y = 2x + 6$ for values of $x$ from $-3$ to 3.

**2** Draw the graph of $2x + 5y = 10$.

**3** Draw the graph of $3x + 2y = 15$.

**4** Draw the graph of $2y = 5x - 8$ for values of $x$ from $-2$ to 4.

**5** Draw the graph of $3x + 4y = 24$.

## EXERCISE 21.3H

**1** Simon had a bath. The graph shows the volume ($V$ gallons) of the water in the bath after $t$ minutes.

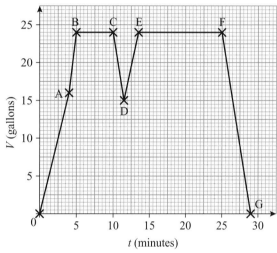

**a)** How many gallons of water are in the bath at A?

**b)** Simon got in the bath at B and out at F. For how long was he in the bath?

**c)** Between 0 and A, the hot tap is on. How many gallons of water per minute came from the hot tap?

**d)** Between A and B, both taps are on. What is the rate of flow of both taps together?
Give your answer in gallons/minute.

**e)** Describe what happened between C and E.

**f)** At what rate did the bath empty? Give your answer in gallons/minute.

**2** A printer's charge for printing programmes is worked out as follows.

A fixed charge of £a
+
$x$ pence per programme for the first 1000 programmes
+
80 pence per programme for each programme over 1000

The graph below shows the total charge for printing up to 1000 programmes.

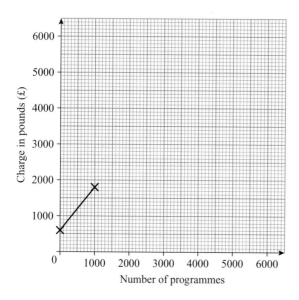

a) What is the fixed charge, £a?
b) Calculate $x$, the charge per programme for the first 1000 programmes.
c) Copy the graph and add a line segment to show the charges for 1000 to 6000 programmes.
d) What is the total charge for 3500 programmes?
e) What is the average cost per programme for 3500 programmes?

**3** The graph shows a train journey.

a) How long did the train journey take?
b) How far was the train journey?
c) How far from the start was the first station?
d) For how long did the train stop at the first station?
e) When was the train travelling fastest?

**4** Water is poured into each of these vessels at a constant rate until they are full.

The following graphs show depth of water ($d$) against time ($t$).

Choose the most suitable graph for each vessel.

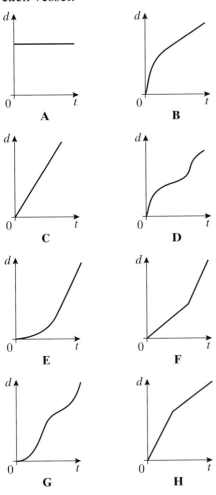

A  B  C  D  E  F  G  H

**5** A mobile phone company offers its customers the choice of two price plans.

| | Plan A | Plan B |
|---|---|---|
| **Monthly subscription** | £10.00 | £s |
| **Free talk time per month** | 60 minutes | 100 minutes |
| **Cost per minute after the free talk time** | a pence | 35 pence |

The graph shows the charges for Plan A and the charges for Plan B up to 100 minutes.

a) Find the monthly subscription for Plan B (£s).

b) Shamir uses price plan B. How much does it cost him if he uses the phone for 250 minutes per month?

c) Copy the graph and add a line to show the cost for Plan B for 100 to 250 minutes.

d) For how many minutes is the cost the same in both price plans?

e) Which price plan is the cheaper when the time for calls is 220 minutes? By how much?

**6** John and Hywel are brothers living in the same house. The graph shows John's cycling trip from their home. He cycles for an hour, stops for a rest, then continues his journey.

**a)** How far did John travel in the first 45 minutes?

**b)** For how many minutes did John rest?

**c)** Hywel sets out from their home at 3 p.m. and travels by car at an average speed of 25 mph on the same route as John. Draw his journey on a copy of the graph.

**d)** Write down the time at which Hywel passes John.

# EXERCISE 21.4H

**1** Which of these functions are quadratic? For each of the functions that is quadratic, state whether the graph is ∪-shaped or ∩-shaped.

**a)** $y = x^2 + 7$    **b)** $y = 2x^3 + x^2 - 4$    **c)** $y = x^2 + x - 7$    **d)** $y = x(6 - x)$

**e)** $y = \dfrac{5}{x^2}$    **f)** $y = x(x^2 + 1)$    **g)** $y = 2x(x + 2)$    **h)** $y = 5 + 3x - x^2$

**2 a)** Copy and complete the table of values for $y = 2x^2$.

| $x$ | $-3$ | $-2$ | $-1$ | 0 | 1 | 2 | 3 |
|---|---|---|---|---|---|---|---|
| $x^2$ | 9 | | | | | 4 | |
| $y = 2x^2$ | 18 | | | | | 8 | |

**b)** Plot the graph of $y = 2x^2$.
Use a scale of 2 cm to 1 unit on the $x$-axis and 1 cm to 1 unit on the $y$-axis.

**c)** Use your graph to
**(i)** find the value of $y$ when $x = -1.8$.    **(ii)** solve $2x^2 = 12$.

**3 a)** Copy and complete the table of values for $y = x^2 + x$.

| $x$ | $-4$ | $-3$ | $-2$ | $-1$ | 0 | 1 | 2 | 3 |
|---|---|---|---|---|---|---|---|---|
| $x^2$ | | | 4 | | | | | 9 |
| $y = x^2 + x$ | | | | | | | | 12 |

**b)** Plot the graph of $y = x^2 + x$.
Use a scale of 2 cm to 1 unit on the $x$-axis and 1 cm to 1 unit on the $y$-axis.

**c)** Use your graph to
(i) find the value of $y$ when $x = 1.6$.      (ii) solve $x^2 + x = 8$.

**4 a)** Copy and complete the table of values for $y = x^2 - x + 2$.

| $x$ | $-3$ | $-2$ | $-1$ | 0 | 1 | 2 | 3 | 4 |
|---|---|---|---|---|---|---|---|---|
| $x^2$ | | 4 | | | | | | 16 |
| $-x$ | | 2 | | | | | | $-4$ |
| 2 | | 2 | | | | | | 2 |
| $y = x^2 - x + 2$ | | 8 | | | | | | 14 |

**b)** Plot the graph of $y = x^2 - x + 2$.
Use a scale of 2 cm to 1 unit on the $x$-axis and 1 cm to 1 unit on the $y$-axis.

**c)** Use your graph to
(i) find the value of $y$ when $x = 0.7$.      (ii) solve $x^2 - x + 2 = 6$.

**5 a)** Copy and complete the table of values for $y = x^2 + 2x - 5$.

| $x$ | $-5$ | $-4$ | $-3$ | $-2$ | $-1$ | 0 | 1 | 2 | 3 |
|---|---|---|---|---|---|---|---|---|---|
| $x^2$ | | | | 4 | | | | | 9 |
| $2x$ | | | | $-4$ | | | | | 6 |
| $-5$ | | | | $-5$ | | | | | $-5$ |
| $y = x^2 + 2x - 5$ | | | | $-5$ | | | | | 10 |

**b)** Plot the graph of $y = x^2 + 2x - 5$.
Use a scale of 2 cm to 1 unit on the $x$-axis and 1 cm to 1 unit on the $y$-axis.

**c)** Use your graph to
(i) find the value of $y$ when $x = -1.4$.      (ii) solve $x^2 + 2x - 5 = 0$.

**6  a)** Copy and complete the table of values for $y = 8 - x^2$.

| $x$ | −3 | −2 | −1 | 0 | 1 | 2 | 3 |
|---|---|---|---|---|---|---|---|
| 8 | | | | 8 | | | 8 |
| $-x^2$ | | | | 0 | | | −9 |
| $y = 8 - x^2$ | | | | 8 | | | −1 |

**b)** Plot the graph of $y = 8 - x^2$.
Use a scale of 2 cm to 1 unit on the $x$-axis and 1 cm to 1 unit on the $y$-axis.

**c)** Use your graph to
  **(i)** find the value of $y$ when $x = 0.5$.      **(ii)** solve $8 - x^2 = -2$.

**7  a)** Copy and complete the table of values for $y = (x - 2)(x + 1)$.

| $x$ | −3 | −2 | −1 | 0 | 1 | 2 | 3 | 4 |
|---|---|---|---|---|---|---|---|---|
| $x - 2$ | | −4 | | | | | 1 | |
| $x + 1$ | | −1 | | | | | 4 | |
| $y = (x - 2)(x + 1)$ | | 4 | | | | | 4 | |

**b)** Plot the graph of $y = (x - 2)(x + 1)$.
Use a scale of 2 cm to 1 unit on the $x$-axis and 1 cm to 1 unit on the $y$-axis.

**c)** Use your graph to
  **(i)** find the minimum value of $y$.      **(ii)** solve $(x - 2)(x + 1) = 2.5$.

**8  a)** Make a table of values for $y = x^2 - 3x + 2$. Choose values of $x$ from −2 to 5.
**b)** Plot the graph of $y = x^2 - 3x + 2$.
Use a scale of 2 cm to 1 unit on the $x$-axis and 1 cm to 1 unit on the $y$-axis.

**c)** Use your graph to solve
  **(i)** $x^2 - 3x + 2 = 1$.      **(ii)** $x^2 - 3x + 2 = 10$.

# EXERCISE 22.1H

**1** Match each of the following angles to its diagram.

295°    45°    168°    25°    90°

**a)**     **b)**

**c)**     **d)**

**e)**

**2** For each angle state whether it is acute, a right angle, obtuse or reflex.

**a)**     **b)**

**c)**     **d)**

**e)**     **f)**

**g)**     **h)**

**3** Are angles of these sizes acute, a right angle, obtuse or reflex?
**a)** 57°          **b)** 110°
**c)** 90°          **d)** 195°
**e)** 28°          **f)** 124°
**g)** 345°         **h)** 91°
**i)** 222°         **j)** 6°

# EXERCISE 22.2H

Work out the size of the unknown angle in each of these diagrams.

# EXERCISE 22.3H

Work out the size of the unknown angle in each of these diagrams.

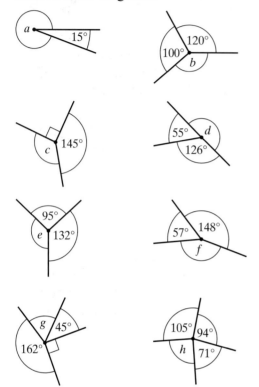

# EXERCISE 22.4H

For each question
- make a copy of the diagram.
- work out the size of each unknown angle.
- give a reason for each answer.

1
125°
b   55°
a

2
150°  c
      d
30°

3
137° f
g  e

4
59°
j   i
  h

5
82°  m
n  k

6
5°     p
    q    r

7
121°
s

8
53°    37°
v  t  u

9
   y  70°
60°
   x  w
   50°

10
   z
z    z

# REVIEW EXERCISE 22H

For each question, first make a copy of the diagram.

**1**

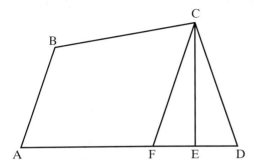

a) Name the line which is perpendicular to AD.
b) Name the line which is parallel to AB.

**2**

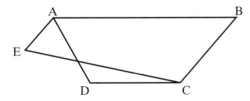

a) Name the line which is parallel to DC.
b) Draw a line through A which is perpendicular to the line EC.

**3**

a) Draw a line through the point D which is perpendicular to AB.
b) Draw a line through the point C which is parallel to AB.

**4**

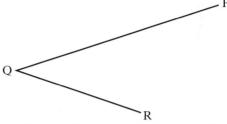

a) Draw a line through the point R which is parallel to the line QP.
b) Draw a line through the point P which is perpendicular to the line QP.

## EXERCISE 23.1H

1 Calculate the angles marked with letters in these triangles.

2 PQR is a triangle. Angle QPR = 48° and angle PQR = 60°.
Sketch the triangle and find angle PRQ.

3 PQR is a triangle. PRS is a straight line. Angle QPR = 48° and angle PQR = 63°.

Calculate angle x.

4 ABCD is a rectangle.
P is halfway between B and C.

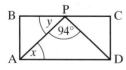

a) What type of triangle is APD?
b) Calculate the angles x and y.

5 In this diagram LM and NP are straight lines.

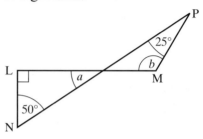

Calculate the size of angles a and b.

## EXERCISE 23.2H

1 Which two of these triangles are congruent?

a)

b)

c)

d)

**2** Which of these triangles are congruent to triangle A?

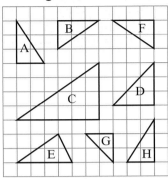

**3** These two triangles are congruent. What is the size of angle $x$?

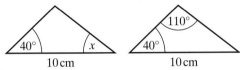

**4** Two triangles are congruent.
One triangle has two angles of 70°.
Write down the size of all three angles in the other triangle.

**5** Draw a rectangle ABCD.
Draw the line AC. This divides the rectangle into two congruent triangles. Label your diagram clearly to show which angles are equal.

**6** Copy and complete these statements.
   **a)** In two congruent triangles, corresponding angles are ………
   **b)** In two congruent triangles, corresponding sides are ………

# EXERCISE 23.3H

**1** Look at these shapes.

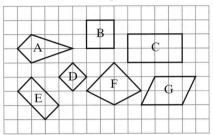

Copy and complete this table. Put a tick (✓) if the description fits. Put a cross (✗) if the description does not fit.

| Shape | All sides equal | Opposite sides parallel | All angles right angles |
|-------|-----------------|-------------------------|-------------------------|
| A     |                 |                         |                         |
| B     |                 |                         |                         |
| C     |                 |                         |                         |
| D     |                 |                         |                         |
| E     |                 |                         |                         |
| F     |                 |                         |                         |
| G     |                 |                         |                         |

**2** Name each of the shapes in question **1**.

**3** **a)** What is the name of a quadrilateral that has two pairs of equal sides which are next to each other?
   **b)** What other fact is true about this quadrilateral?

**4** Sketch a trapezium. Label clearly any equal sides and any parallel sides.

**5** A quadrilateral has opposite sides equal and parallel.
Name all the different shapes this quadrilateral could be.

# EXERCISE 23.4H

**1** Here are some shapes made out of centimetre squares.

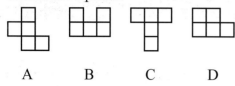

A     B     C     D

Which ones will not fold up to make an open box?

**2** A box has edges of length 5 cm, 6 cm and 3 cm.
Is it a cube or a cuboid? Explain your answer.

**3** Draw a net of this closed box.
Label the length of each edge.

# EXERCISE 23.5H

These solid shapes are made from centimetre cubes.
Use isometric paper to draw the shapes.

**1**      **2**

**3**      **4**

**5**      **6**

## EXERCISE 24.1H

1   Name these parts of a circle.

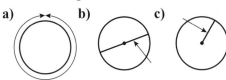

a)       b)       c)

2   Name these polygons.

a)       b)       c)

3   A regular hexagon is constructed in a circle.
    How many degrees are measured at the centre to draw each radius required?

4   Draw a circle of radius 5 cm and use it to construct a regular pentagon.
    Measure the length of a side of your pentagon.

5   Draw a circle of radius 6 cm and use it to construct a regular nine-sided polygon.
    Measure the length of a side of your polygon.

6

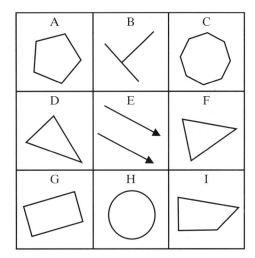

Copy and complete the following table to show which of the above boxes contains:

| a circle | H |
| --- | --- |
| two parallel lines | |
| an isosceles triangle | |
| a pentagon | |
| a rectangle | |

**7** In each of parts **a)**, **b)** and **c)** a diagram of one of the named shapes has been drawn. Copy these diagrams and draw the other named shape, showing clearly the difference between the two shapes.

   **a)**   A square and a rectangle.

   **b)**   An isosceles triangle and an equilateral triangle.

   **c)**   An octogon and a pentagon.

**8** Copy the following diagrams and draw lines to show

   **an arc of a circle**
   **a radius of a circle**
   **a tangent of a circle**
   **a diameter of a circle**
   **a chord of a circle**

   An arc of a circle has been draw for you.

| | |
|---|---|
| Arc | ⊙ |
| Radius | ⊙ |
| Tangent | ⊙ |
| Diameter | ⊙ |
| Chord | ⊙ |

## EXERCISE 25.1H

1 This graph converts feet to centimetres.
   Use the graph to find how many
   **a)** centimetres is 6 feet.
   **b)** feet is 250 cm.
   **c)** centimetres is 1 foot.

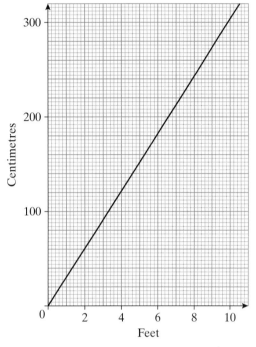

2 Area of land used to be measured in acres. It is now measured in hectares (ha).
   One hectare is 10 000 m². The graph converts between acres and hectares.

Use the graph to find how many
**a)** hectares is 100 acres.    **b)** acres is 45 ha.    **c)** acres is 1 ha.

# EXERCISE 25.2H

1   Mr Smith is paying back a loan over a number of years.
The graph shows how much he owes.

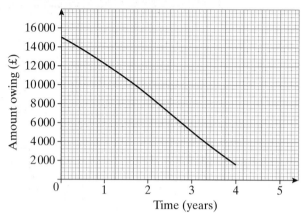

a)   How much did Mr Smith borrow?
b)   How much did he owe after
     **(i)** 2 years?        **(ii)** 4 years?
c)   If he keeps on paying the money back at the same rate, when will he owe nothing?
     Give your answer to the nearest month.

2   The graph shows a patient's temperature over a day.

a)   When was the patient's temperature highest?
b)   What was the temperature at 15:00?
c)   How often was the patient's temperature taken?
d)   Why are the points joined with a dotted line?

3. The graph shows the temperature of the water in a kettle, as it is heated.
   a) After how many seconds is the water over 80 °C?
   b) What is the temperature after 50 seconds?
   c) How much does the temperature increase between 20 seconds and 40 seconds?

# EXERCISE 25.3H

1. Jack is walking from Church Stretton to Ratlinghope across the Long Mynd, a hill in Shropshire.
   His journey is shown on the graph.
   Describe each of the four stages of Jack's journey.

2. Jasbir and Robert have a race over 2 km.
   Robert runs, then walks and then runs again.
   Jasbir jogs at a steady speed.
   The graph shows what happened.
   a) Whose graph is the broken line?
   b) Who won the race?
   c) Describe what happened when the lines cross.

3. The graph shows two trains travelling between Leicester and St Pancras.
   The distance between the stations is 100 miles.
   a) When did train B leave Leicester?
   b) Which train stopped? How far from St Pancras was it when it stopped?
   c) Find the time and distance from St Pancras when the trains passed each other.

4   The graph shows Sue's journey by car from her home in Swansea to a service area and
    then on to Cheltenham, which is 120 miles from Swansea.
    a)  How far did Sue travel in the first hour?
    b)  For how many minutes did Sue stay at the service area?
    c)  Without calculating any speeds, explain how you can tell whether Sue was, on
        average, travelling faster before or after her stop.
    d)  Louise sets out from Cheltenham at 10.30 a.m. and travels at an average speed of
        40 mph to the service area. Draw her journey on a copy of the graph.

## EXERCISE 26.1H

Find the size of the lettered angles. Give a reason for each answer.

**1**

**2**

**3**

**4**

**5**

**6**

**7**

**8**

**9**

**10**

## EXERCISE 26.2H

Find the size of the lettered angles. Give a reason for each answer.

**1**

**2**

**3**

**4**

## EXERCISE 26.3H

**1** Name each of these quadrilaterals.

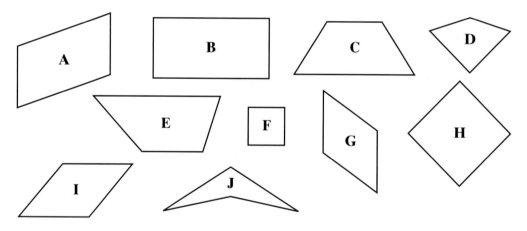

**2** Name the quadrilateral or quadrilaterals which have the following properties.
   **a)** Four right angles
   **b)** Both pairs of opposite sides parallel
   **c)** Equal diagonals
   **d)** At least one pair of opposite sides parallel
   **e)** Diagonals that bisect each other

3   Plot each set of points on squared paper and join them in order to make quadrilateral.
    Use a different grid for each part.
    Write down the special name of each quadrilateral.
    a)  (3, 0), (5, 2), (3, 4), (1, 2)
    b)  (2, 1), (4, 1), (4, 5), (2, 5)
    c)  (1, 2), (3, 1), (3, 6), (1, 7)
    d)  (2, 1), (2, 5), (8, 4), (8, 2)

4   A rhombus is a special type of parallelogram.
    What extra properties does a rhombus have?

5   A quadrilateral has angles of 80°, 100°, 80°, 100° in order as you work your way
    around the quadrilateral. The sides are not all the same length.
    Which special quadrilateral could have these as its angles?
    Draw the quadrilateral and mark on the angles.

# EXERCISE 26.4H

1   A polygon has nine sides.
    Work out the sum of the interior angles of this polygon.

2   A polygon has 13 sides.
    Work out the sum of the interior angles of this polygon.

3   Four of the exterior angles of a hexagon are 93°, 50°, 37° and 85°.
    The other two angles are equal.
    a)  Work out the size of these equal exterior angles.
    b)  Work out the size of the interior angles of the hexagon.

4   Four of the interior angles of a pentagon are 170°, 80°, 157° and 75°.
    a)  Work out the size of the other interior angle.
    b)  Work out the size of the exterior angles of the pentagon.

5   A regular polygon has 18 sides.
    Find the size of the exterior and the interior angles of this polygon.

6   A regular polygon has 24 sides.
    Find the size of the exterior and the interior angles of this polygon.

7   A regular polygon has an exterior angle of 12°.
    Work out the number of sides that the polygon has.

8   A regular polygon has an interior angle of 172°.
    Work out the number of sides that the polygon has.

## EXERCISE 27.1H

1   Measure the length of each of these lines in centimetres.

a) ————————————————————————

b) ————————

c) ——————————————————

d) ——————————

e) ————————————————————

2   Measure the length of each of these objects.

a)

b)

3   Measure the length of each side of these shapes.

a)                                          b)

# EXERCISE 27.2H

Copy and complete this table.
Estimate each angle first and then
measure it with a protractor.

| Angle | Estimated size | Measured size |
|-------|----------------|---------------|
| a     |                |               |
| b     |                |               |
| c     |                |               |
| d     |                |               |
| e     |                |               |
| f     |                |               |
| g     |                |               |
| h     |                |               |
| i     |                |               |
| j     |                |               |

# EXERCISE 27.3H

**1**  Draw accurately each of these angles.

**a)**

**b)**

**c)**

**2**  Draw accurately each of these angles.

**a)**  70°           **b)**  45°           **c)**  151°           **d)**  67°

**e)**  139°          **f)**  28°           **g)**  80°            **h)**  113°

**3**  Draw accurately each of these reflex angles.

**a)**  210°          **b)**  300°          **c)**  188°           **d)**  275°

# EXERCISE 27.4H

**1**  Make an accurate full-size drawing of each of these triangles.
For each triangle, measure the unknown length and angles from your drawing.

**a)**

**b)**

**c)**  Triangle ABC where AB = 8 cm, angle BAC = 58° and AC = 5 cm

**2**  Make an accurate full-size drawing of each of these triangles.
For each triangle, measure the unknown lengths and angle from your drawing.

**a)**

**b)**

**c)**  Triangle XYZ where YZ = 6.5 cm, angle XZY = 67° and angle ZYX = 43°

# EXERCISE 27.5H

**1** Make an accurate full-size drawing of each of these triangles.
For each triangle, measure all the angles from your drawing.

**a)**

**b)**

**c)** Triangle ABC where AB = 6 cm, BC = 6.5 cm and AC = 7 cm

**2** Make an accurate full-size drawing of each of these triangles.
For each triangle, measure the unknown length and angles from your drawing.

**a)**

**b)**

**c)** Triangle XYZ where YZ = 6.8 cm, angle XZY = 42° and XY = 8 cm

# EXERCISE 27.6H

**1** Measure each of these lines as accurately as possible.
Using the scales given, work out the actual length that each line represents.

| | |
|---|---|
| **a)** ─────────────── | 1 cm to 6 m |
| **b)** ─────────── | 1 cm to 20 km |
| **c)** ─────────────── | 2 cm to 5 miles |
| **d)** ────────── | 1 cm to 4 m |

**2** Use the scales given to draw accurately lines to represent these lengths.
   **a)** 6 m          Scale: 1 cm to 1 m
   **b)** 8 km         Scale: 1 cm to 2 km
   **c)** 15 miles     Scale: 3 cm to 5 miles
   **d)** 450 m        Scale: 1 cm to 100 m

**3** Here is a plan of a bedroom.
The scale of the drawing is
1 cm to 50 cm.

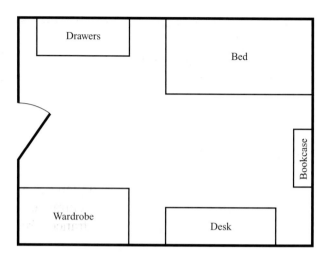

a) Work out the actual length and width of the bedroom.
b) Work out the actual length and width of each of the five items in the bedroom.
c) The window in the bedroom measures 1 m by 1 m 75 cm.
   What will the measurements of the window be on this scale drawing?

**4** The map shows some towns and cities in Scotland.
The scale of the map is 1 cm to 10 km.

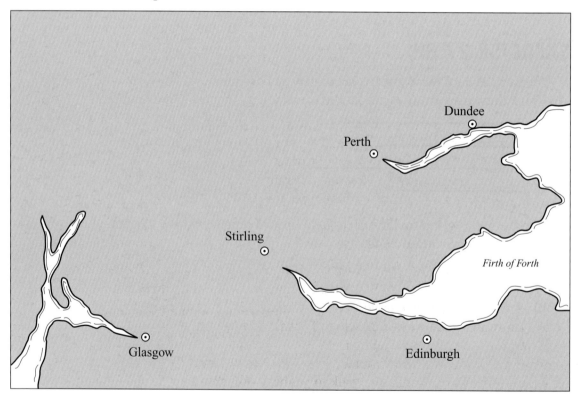

a) What is the real-life distance, in kilometres, between these towns?
    **(i)**  Glasgow and Stirling          **(ii)**  Edinburgh and Glasgow
    **(iii)** Edinburgh and Perth          **(iv)** Glasgow and Dundee
    **(v)**  Perth and Dundee           **(vi)** Edinburgh and Stirling
b) It is 660 km from Edinburgh to London.
   How many centimetres will this be on the map?

# EXERCISE 27.7H

**1**   The diagram shows a section of a plan of a school. From a point P in the playground
the plan shows the position of the entrances to various schoolrooms.
Find the bearing of each of the entrances from the point P.
The scale of the map is 1 cm to 10 m.
Find the actual distance of each of the entrances from P.

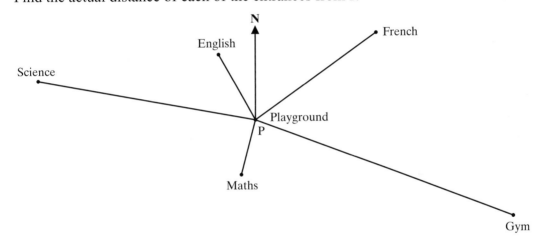

**2**   Three towns are Delham, Easton and Fanbury.
Easton is 3 miles from Delham on a bearing of 065°.
Fanbury is $2\frac{1}{2}$ miles from Delham on a bearing of 290°.
Make a scale drawing showing these three towns.
Use a scale of 2 cm to 1 mile.

**3**   Jenny went for a walk.
She started from home (H) and walked 500 m on a bearing of 150° to the zoo (Z).
From the zoo she walked 900 m on a bearing of 088° to the café (C).
From the café she walked 600 m on a bearing of 350° to the shop (S).
a) Draw an accurate scale drawing of Jenny's walk.
   Use a scale of 1 cm to 100 m.
b) How far is Jenny from home?
c) On what bearing must she walk to get back home?

## EXERCISE 28.1H

1   Two points, A and B, are 7 cm apart.
    Draw the locus of points that are
    equidistant from A and B.

2   A badger will never go further than
    3 miles from its home.
    Draw a scale diagram to show the
    regions where the badger might go
    looking for food.

3   Draw an equilateral triangle, ABC, of
    side 6 cm.
    Shade the region of points inside the
    triangle which are nearer to AB than
    to AC.

4   A rectangular garden measures 8 m by
    6 m. A fence is built from F, at a right
    angle across the garden.
    Draw a scale diagram and construct
    the line of the fence.

5   Draw a square, ABCD, of side 5 cm.
    Draw the locus of points inside the
    square which are more than 3 cm
    from A.

6   Zeke is walking across a field.
    He notices a bull starting to chase after
    him. He runs the shortest distance to
    the hedge.
    Copy the diagram and draw the path
    that Zeke runs.

• Zeke

7   Draw a rectangle, PQRS, with sides
    PQ = 7 cm and QR = 5 cm.
    Shade the region of points that are
    closer to P than to Q.

8   Draw an angle of 80°.
    Construct the bisector of the angle.

9   An office is a rectangle measuring
    16 m by 12 m. There are two
    electricity points in the office at
    opposite corners of the room. The
    vacuum cleaner has a wire 10 m long.
    Make a scale drawing to show how
    much of the room can be cleaned.

10  Make another scale drawing of the
    office in question 9.
    Shade the locus of points which are
    equidistant from the two electricity
    points.
    Use this locus to work out the length
    of wire needed for the vacuum cleaner
    to reach everywhere in the office.

# EXERCISE 28.2H

**1** Draw a point and label it P.
Draw the region of points that are less
than 4 cm from P and more than 6 cm
from P.

**2** A rectangular garden measures 20 m
by 12 m.
A tree is to be planted so that it is more
than 4 m from each corner of the garden.
Make a scale drawing to find the area
where the tree can be planted.

**3** Two points, A and B, are 5 cm apart.
Find the region that is less than 3 cm
from A and more than 4 cm from B.

**4** Make an accurate drawing of a
triangle, PQR, where PQ = 6 cm,
P = 40° and Q = 35°.
Find the point X, which is 2 cm from
R and equidistant from P and Q.

**5** Two coastguard stations, A and B, are
20 km apart on a straight coastline.
The coastguard at A knows that a ship
is within 15 km of him.
The coastguard at B knows that the
same ship is within 10 km of him.
Make a scale drawing to show the
region where the ship could be.

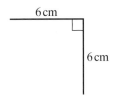

**6** Two lines, each 6 cm long, join to
form a right angle.
Draw the region of points which are
less than 3 cm from these lines.

**7** Two points, P and Q, are 7 cm apart.
Find the points which are the same
distance from P and Q and are also
within 5 cm of Q.

**8** The diagram shows three coastguard
stations, C, D and E.
A ship is within 25 km of C and closer
to DE than DC.
Find the region where the ship could be.

**9** A garden is a rectangle, ABCD, with
AB = 5 m and BC = 3 m.
A new flowerbed is to be made in the
garden.
It must be more than 2 m from A and
less than 1.5 m from CD.
Make a scale drawing to show where
the flowerbed could be.

**10** EFG is a triangle with EF = 6 cm,
FG = 8 cm and EG = 10 cm.
Draw the perpendicular from F to EG.
Indicate the points on this line that are
more than 7 cm from G.

# EXERCISE 29.1H

1  Copy these shapes.
   On each shape, draw the lines of
   symmetry.

2  How many lines of symmetry do these
   arrows have?

3  Draw a rectangle.
   A rectangle has two lines of symmetry.
   Draw both lines of symmetry on your
   rectangle.

4  This triangle has three lines of
   symmetry.
   What type of triangle is it?

5  Copy this grid.
   Shade more squares so that the diagonal
   broken line is a line of symmetry.

6  Copy this grid.
   Shade more squares so that the grid
   has two lines of symmetry shown by
   the dotted lines.

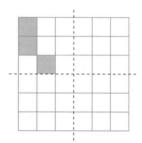

7  Make a pattern
   with two lines
   of symmetry.
   Shade squares on
   a grid like this.

8  Copy these diagrams.
   Complete the diagrams so that the
   broken lines are lines of symmetry.

a)    b)

c)

# EXERCISE 29.2H

1   What is the order of rotation symmetry of each of these shapes?

a)

b)

c)

d)

2   Look at this regular pentagon.

How many lines of symmetry does it have?
What is its order of rotation symmetry?

3   This triangle has rotation symmetry of order 3.

Draw a different triangle that has no rotation symmetry.

4   Copy this grid.
Shade more squares so that the pattern has rotation symmetry of order 2.

5   Copy this grid.
Shade more squares so that the pattern has rotation symmetry of order 4.

6   Shade squares on a 3 × 3 grid so that your pattern has rotation symmetry of order 2 but no reflection symmetry.

7   Copy this diagram.

Complete it so that it has rotation symmetry of order 4.

8   Copy this diagram.

Complete it so that it has rotation symmetry of order 3, but no reflection symmetry.

9   Draw a simple pattern that has rotation symmetry of order 2.

# EXERCISE 29.3H

1   Copy each shape on to squared paper
    and reflect it in the mirror line shown.

a)

b)

c)

d)

e)

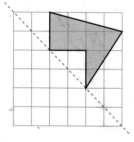

2   Copy each pair of shapes on to
    squared paper and draw the mirror line
    for the reflection.

a)

b)

c)

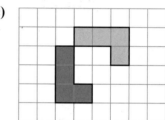

3   Copy the diagram.
    Reflect flag A in the mirror line. Label
    the image B.
    Reflect flag A in the y-axis. Label the
    image C.

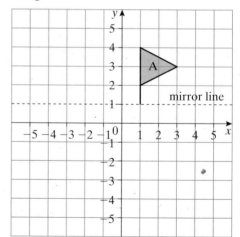

**4**  Draw *x*- and *y*-axes from −5 to 5.
Plot the points (2, 1), (5, 1), (5, 3)
and (3, 5).
Join the points to form a trapezium.
Label it A.
Reflect shape A in the *y*-axis. Label
the image B.
Reflect shape A in the *x*-axis. Label
the image C.

**5**  Through what angle is the darker
object rotated to fit the lighter image?

**a)**

**b)**

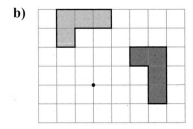

**6**  Points A, B and C are part of this shape.
It has rotation symmetry of order 6.

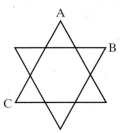

What clockwise angle of rotation maps
**a)**  A on to B?
**b)**  A on to C?

**7**  Triangle A has been rotated or
reflected to give these image triangles.

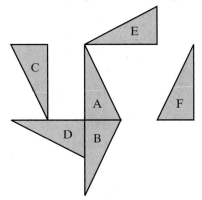

**a)**  List the triangles which are
reflections of triangle A.
**b)**  List the triangles which are
rotations of triangle A.

## EXERCISE 30.1H

**1**  Draw a pair of axes and label them
   −2 to 4 for *x* and *y*.
   **a)**  Draw a triangle with vertices at
      (1, 1), (1, 3) and (0, 3). Label it A.
   **b)**  Reflect triangle A in the line $x = 2$.
      Label it B.
   **c)**  Reflect triangle A in the line $y = x$.
      Label it C.
   **d)**  Reflect triangle A in the line $y = 2$.
      Label it D.

**2**  Draw a pair of axes and label them
   −3 to 3 for *x* and *y*.
   **a)**  Draw a triangle with vertices at
      (−1, 1), (−1, 3) and (−2, 3).
      Label it A.
   **b)**  Reflect triangle A in the line $x = \frac{1}{2}$.
      Label it B.
   **c)**  Reflect triangle A in the line $y = x$.
      Label it C.
   **d)**  Reflect triangle A in the line
      $y = -x$. Label it D.

**3**  For each part
   • copy the diagram, making it larger if
     you wish.
   • reflect the shape in the mirror line.
   **a)**

**b)**

**c)**

**4**  Describe fully the single
   transformation that maps
   **a)**  shape A on to shape B.
   **b)**  shape A on to shape C.
   **c)**  shape B on to shape D.

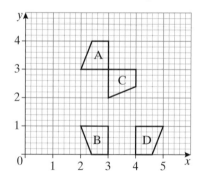

**5** Describe fully the single transformation that maps
   a) triangle A on to triangle B.
   b) triangle A on to triangle C.
   c) triangle E on to triangle F.

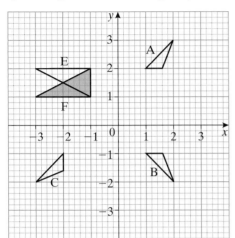

# EXERCISE 30.2H

**1** Copy the diagram.
   a) Rotate trapezium A through 180° about the origin. Label it B.
   b) Rotate trapezium A through 90° clockwise about the point (0, 1). Label it C.
   c) Rotate trapezium A through 90° anticlockwise about the point (−1, 1). Label it D.

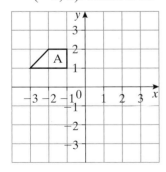

**2** Copy the diagram.
   a) Rotate flag A through 90° clockwise about the origin. Label it B.
   b) Rotate flag A through 90° anticlockwise about the point (1, −1). Label it C.
   c) Rotate flag A through 180° about the point (0, −1) Label it D.

**3** Draw a pair of axes and label them −4 to 4 for x and y.
   a) Draw a triangle with vertices (1, 1), (2, 1) and (2, 3). Label it A.
   b) Rotate triangle A through 90° anticlockwise about the origin. Label it B.
   c) Rotate triangle A through 180° about the point (2, 1). Label it C.
   d) Rotate triangle A through 90° clockwise about the point (−2, 1). Label it D.

**4** Copy the diagram. Rotate the triangle through 180° about the point C.

**5** Copy the diagram. Rotate the shape through 90° clockwise about the point O.

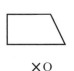

**6** Copy the diagram. Rotate the flag through 150° clockwise about the point A.

A •

**7** Describe fully the single transformation that maps
a) trapezium A on to trapezium B.
b) trapezium A on to trapezium C.
c) trapezium A on to trapezium D.

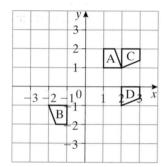

**8** Describe fully the single transformation that maps
a) flag A on to flag B.
b) flag A on to flag C.
c) flag A on to flag D.

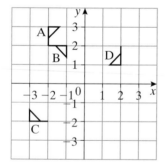

**9** Describe fully the single transformation that maps triangle A on to triangle B.

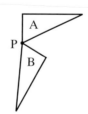

**10** Describe fully the single transformation that maps
a) triangle A on to triangle B.
b) triangle A on to triangle C.
c) triangle A on to triangle D.
d) triangle A on to triangle E.
e) triangle A on to triangle F.
Hint: Some of these transformations are reflections.

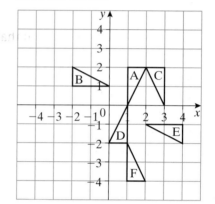

# EXERCISE 30.3H

**1** Draw a pair of axes and label them −2 to 6 for $x$ and $y$.
a) Draw a triangle with vertices at (1, 1), (1, 2), and (4, 1). Label it A.
b) Translate triangle A by vector $\begin{pmatrix} 1 \\ 3 \end{pmatrix}$. Label it B.
c) Translate triangle A by vector $\begin{pmatrix} -3 \\ 4 \end{pmatrix}$. Label it C.
d) Translate triangle A by vector $\begin{pmatrix} -2 \\ -3 \end{pmatrix}$. Label it D.

**2** Draw a pair of axes and label them −3 to 5 for $x$ and $y$.
a) Draw a triangle with vertices at (2, 1), (2, 3) and (3, 1). Label it A.

**b)** Translate triangle A by vector $\begin{pmatrix} 2 \\ 1 \end{pmatrix}$.
Label it B.

**c)** Translate triangle A by vector $\begin{pmatrix} -5 \\ -3 \end{pmatrix}$.
Label it C.

**d)** Translate triangle A by vector $\begin{pmatrix} 2 \\ -4 \end{pmatrix}$.
Label it D.

**3** Describe the single transformation that maps
**a)** triangle A on to triangle B.
**b)** triangle A on to triangle C.
**c)** triangle A on to triangle D.
**d)** triangle B on to triangle D.

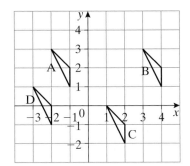

**4** Describe the single transformation that maps
**a)** shape A on to shape B.
**b)** shape A on to shape C.
**c)** shape A on to shape D.
**d)** shape D on to shape E.
**e)** shape A on to shape F.
**f)** shape E on to shape G.
**g)** shape B on to shape H.
**h)** shape H on to shape F.
Hint: Not all the transformations are translations.

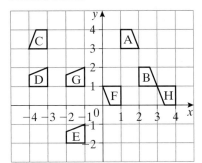

# 31 → ENLARGEMENTS

## EXERCISE 31.1H

1   For each of these shapes
    • copy the shape on to squared paper.
    • draw an enlargement of the shape
      using the scale factor given.

   a)   Scale factor 2

   b)   Scale factor 3

   c)   Scale factor 3

   d)   Scale factor 2

   e)   Scale factor 2

2   Work out the scale factor of
    enlargement of each of these pairs of
    shapes.

   a)

   b)

   c)

**d)**

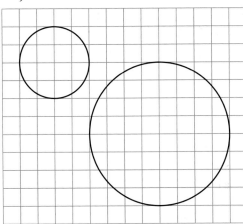

3   For each of these pairs of shapes, is the larger shape an enlargement of the smaller shape?
Give a reason for your answers.

**a)**

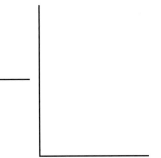

**b)**

# EXERCISE 31.2H

1 Copy each of the shapes on to squared paper.
Enlarge each of them by the scale factor given.
Use the dot as the centre of the enlargement.

**a)** Scale factor 3

**b)** Scale factor 2

**c)** Scale factor 4

**d)** Scale factor 3

**e)** Scale factor 2

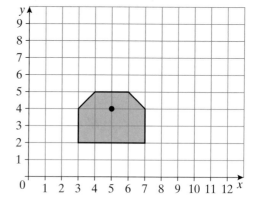

**2** Copy each of these diagrams on to squared paper.
For each of these diagrams find
**(i)** the scale factor of the enlargement.
**(ii)** the coordinates of the centre of the enlargement.

**a)**

**b)**

**c)**

**d)**

**e)**

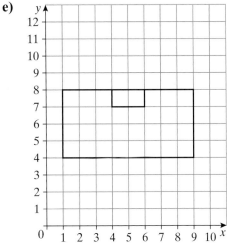

# EXERCISE 31.3H

1 Draw a pair of axes and label them 0 to 6 for both $x$ and $y$.
 a) Draw a triangle with vertices at (0, 6), (3, 6) and (3, 3). Label it A.
 b) Enlarge triangle A by scale factor $\frac{1}{3}$, with the origin as the centre of enlargement. Label it B.
 c) Describe fully the single transformation that maps triangle B on to triangle A.

2 Draw a pair of axes and label them 0 to 6 for both $x$ and $y$.
 a) Draw a triangle with vertices at (5, 2), (5, 6) and (3, 6). Label it A.
 b) Enlarge triangle A by scale factor $\frac{1}{2}$, with centre of enlargement (3, 2). Label it B.
 c) Describe fully the single transformation that maps triangle B on to triangle A.

3 Draw a pair of axes and label them 0 to 8 for both $x$ and $y$.
 a) Draw a triangle with vertices at (2, 1), (2, 3), (3, 2). Label it A.
 b) Enlarge triangle A by scale factor $2\frac{1}{2}$, with the origin as the centre of enlargement. Label it B.
 c) Describe fully the single transformation that maps triangle B on to triangle A.

4 Draw a pair of axes and label them 0 to 7 for both $x$ and $y$.
 a) Draw a trapezium with vertices at (1, 2), (1, 3), (2, 3) and (3, 2). Label it A.
 b) Enlarge trapezium A by scale factor 3, with centre of enlargement (1, 2). Label it B.
 c) Describe fully the single transformation that maps trapezium B on to trapezium A.

5 Describe fully the single transformation that maps
 a) triangle A on to triangle B.
 b) triangle B on to triangle A.
 c) triangle A on to triangle C.
 d) triangle C on to triangle A.

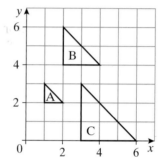

Hint: in questions 6, 7 and 8, not all the transformations are enlargements.

6 Describe fully the single transformation that maps
 a) flag A on to flag B.
 b) flag B on to flag C.
 c) flag B on to flag D.
 d) flag B on to flag E.
 e) flag F on to flag G.

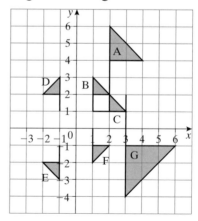

7  Draw a pair of axes and label them $-4$ to 4 for $x$ and $y$.
   a) Draw a triangle with vertices at $(2, 1)$, $(2, 2)$ and $(4, 2)$. Label it A.
   b) Reflect triangle A in the line $y = 0$. Label it B.
   c) Reflect triangle A in the line $x = 1$. Label it C.
   d) Rotate triangle B by $90°$ anticlockwise about the origin. Label it D.
   e) Enlarge triangle A by scale factor $\frac{1}{2}$, with the origin as the centre of enlargement. Label it E.

8  Copy the diagram.
   a) Rotate shape A through $90°$ clockwise about the origin. Label it B.
   b) Rotate shape A through $180°$ about $(2, 2)$. Label it C.
   c) Enlarge shape A by scale factor $\frac{1}{2}$, with centre of enlargement $(-2, 0)$. Label it D.

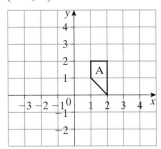

## EXERCISE 32.1H

**1** What are the readings on this scale?

a)        b)   c)

**2** What is the reading on this scale?

**3** What are the readings on this thermometer?

**4** How long is this nail?

**5** Measure the distance from A to B.

A                                                    B

## EXERCISE 32.2H

**1** Change these lengths to centimetres.
  **a)**  2 m            **b)**  3.5 m
  **c)**  20 mm        **d)**  15 m
  **e)**  45 mm

**2** Change these lengths to millimetres.
  **a)**  2 cm          **b)**  5.5 cm
  **c)**  10 cm        **d)**  2 m
  **e)**  3.5 m

**3** Change these weights to grams.
  **a)**  2 kg           **b)**  5 kg
  **c)**  6.35 kg      **d)**  0.8 kg
  **e)**  0.525 kg

**4** Put these volumes in order, smallest first.

    1.2 litres        500 ml        2 litres
    2500 ml        800 cl

**5** Which metric units would you use to measure these lengths?
   a) The span of your hand
   b) The length of a corridor
   c) The width of a window
   d) The distance you can walk in a day
   e) The distance from London to Edinburgh

**6** Put these weights in order, smallest first.

   1.2 kg          1500 g          160 g
   2000 g          0.8 kg

**7** Change these volumes to millilitres.
   a) 2 litres          b) 3.5 litres
   c) 2 cl              d) 15 cl
   e) 0.345 litres

**8** Graham has three pieces of string. The lengths are 45 cm, 85 mm and 1.2 m.
   a) Write them down in order, shortest first.
   b) What is the total length of string
      (i)   in millimetres?
      (ii)  in centimetres?
      (iii) in metres?

# EXERCISE 32.3H

Here are some approximate conversions between imperial and metric units.

| Length | Weight |
|---|---|
| 8 km ≈ 5 miles | 1 kg ≈ 2.2 pounds (lb) |
| 1 m ≈ 40 inches | |
| 1 inch ≈ 2.5 cm | **Capacity** |
| 1 foot (ft) ≈ 30 cm | 4 litres ≈ 7 pints (pt) |

**1** Change these imperial measures to the approximate metric equivalent.
   a) 6 feet      b) 35 miles   c) 14 lb
   d) 45 lb       e) 14 pints

**2** Change these metric measures to the approximate imperial equivalent.
   a) 24 km      b) 5 m        c) 5 kg
   d) 12 litres  e) 20 cm

**3** Stephen needs 1 pound of meat for a recipe.
   How many grams should he buy?

**4** A radiator is 20 inches wide.
   What is this in centimetres?

**5** Cola is sold in 2 litre bottles.
   How much is this in pints?

**6** Pauline is 5 foot 4 inches tall.
   What is this in centimetres?

**7** a) A baby weighs 3.8 kilograms.
      Calculate the approximate weight of the baby in pounds.
   b) 1.75 pints is approximately equal to 1 litre.
      A container holds 56 pints of paraffin.
      Calculate the approximate volume of the paraffin in litres.

**8** Mark drives towards Nottingham and sees this sign.

   | Grantham | 23 miles |
   | Nottingham | 53 miles |

   Roughly how far is it, in kilometres, from Grantham to Nottingham if Mark has to drive through Grantham to get to Nottingham?

# EXERCISE 32.4H

1   Estimate the following.
    a)  The height your desk
    b)  The width of a door
    c)  The mass of a glass of water
    d)  The capacity of a kitchen sink
    e)  The distance you can walk in an
        hour

2   Estimate the height of this lamp post.

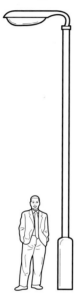

3   The building in this picture is about
    16 m high.
    Estimate the height of the lorry.

4   Alan wants to estimate the length of
    his bedroom. His foot is 20 cm long.
    He works out that the room is 16 foot
    lengths long.
    What is his estimate of the length of
    his bedroom?

5   Adrian is asked to estimate the
    distance he walks to school.
    His answer is 1.135 km.
    a)  Why is this not a sensible
        estimate?
    b)  What would be a better estimate?

# 33 → MEASURES 2

## EXERCISE 33.1H

1   Change these measures to the units shown.
   **a)**  25 cm to mm
   **b)**  24 m to cm
   **c)**  1.36 cm to mm
   **d)**  15.1 cm to mm
   **e)**  0.235 m to mm

2   Change these measures to the units shown.
   **a)**  $2 \text{ m}^2$ to $\text{cm}^2$
   **b)**  $3 \text{ cm}^2$ to $\text{mm}^2$
   **c)**  $1.12 \text{ m}^2$ to $\text{cm}^2$
   **d)**  $0.05 \text{ cm}^2$ to $\text{mm}^2$
   **e)**  $2 \text{ m}^2$ to $\text{mm}^2$

3   Change these measures to the units shown.
   **a)**  $8000 \text{ mm}^2$ to $\text{cm}^2$
   **b)**  $84\,000 \text{ mm}^2$ to $\text{cm}^2$
   **c)**  $2\,000\,000 \text{ cm}^2$ to $\text{m}^2$
   **d)**  $18\,000\,000 \text{ cm}^2$ to $\text{m}^2$
   **e)**  $64\,000 \text{ cm}^2$ to $\text{m}^2$

4   Change these measures to the units shown.
   **a)**  $32 \text{ cm}^3$ to $\text{mm}^3$
   **b)**  $24 \text{ m}^3$ to $\text{cm}^3$
   **c)**  $5.2 \text{ cm}^3$ to $\text{mm}^3$
   **d)**  $0.42 \text{ m}^3$ to $\text{cm}^3$
   **e)**  $0.02 \text{ cm}^3$ to $\text{mm}^3$

5   Change these measures to the units shown.
   **a)**  $5\,200\,000 \text{ cm}^3$ to $\text{m}^3$
   **b)**  $270\,000 \text{ mm}^3$ to $\text{cm}^3$
   **c)**  $210 \text{ cm}^3$ to $\text{m}^3$
   **d)**  $8.4 \text{ m}^3$ to $\text{mm}^3$
   **e)**  $170 \text{ mm}^3$ to $\text{cm}^3$

6   Change these measures to the units shown.
   **a)**  $36$ litres to $\text{cm}^3$
   **b)**  6300 ml to litres
   **c)**  1.4 litres to ml
   **d)**  61 ml to litres
   **e)**  $5400 \text{ cm}^3$ to litres

## EXERCISE 33.2H

1   Copy and complete each of these statements.

   **a)**  A length given as 4.3 cm, to 1 decimal place, is between ............ cm and ............ cm.

   **b)**  A capacity given as 463 ml, to the nearest millilitre, is between ............ ml and ............ ml.

   **c)**  A time given as 10.5 seconds, to the nearest tenth of a second, is between ............ seconds and ............ seconds.

**d)** A mass given as 78 kg, to the nearest kilogram, is between ............ kg and ............ kg.

**e)** An area given as 5.5 m², to 1 decimal place, is between ............ m² and ............ m².

**2** The number of people attending a football match was given as 24 000, to the nearest thousand.
What was the least number of people that could have been at the match?

**3** Kerry measures her height as 142 cm, to the nearest centimetre.
Write down the two values between which her height must lie.

**4** The height of a desk is stated as 75.0 cm, to 1 decimal place.
Write down the two values between which its height must lie.

**5** Rashid measures the thickness of a piece of plywood as 7.83 mm, to 2 decimal places.
Write down the two values between which its thickness must lie.

**6** The sides of this triangle are given in centimetres, correct to 1 decimal place.

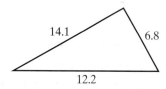

**a)** Write down the shortest and longest possible length of each side.

**b)** Write down the shortest and longest possible length of the perimeter.

**7** John has two pieces of string. He measures them as 125 mm and 182 mm, to the nearest millimetre. He puts the two pieces end to end. What is the shortest and longest that their combined lengths can be?

**8** Mel and Mary both buy some apples. Mel buys 3.5 kg and Mary buys 4.2 kg. Both weights are correct to the nearest tenth of a kilogram.
**a)** What is the smallest possible difference between the amounts they have bought?
**b)** What is the largest possible difference between the amounts they have bought?

# EXERCISE 33.3H

**1** Rewrite each of these statements using sensible values for the measurements.
**a)** My mass is 78.32 kg.
**b)** It takes Katriona 16 minutes and 15.6 seconds to walk to school.
**c)** The distance to London from Sheffield is 161.64 miles.
**d)** The length of our classroom is 5 metres 14 cm 3 mm.
**e)** My water jug hold 3.02 litres.

**2** Give your answer to each of these questions to a sensible degree of accuracy.
**a)** Estimate the length of this line.

**b)** Estimate the size of this angle.

**c)** A rectangle is 2.3 cm long and 4.5 cm wide. Find the area of the rectangle.

**d)** The diameter of a circle is 8 cm. Calculate its circumference.

**e)** The volume of a cube is 7 cm³. Find the length of an edge.

**f)** An angle in a pie chart is found by working out $\frac{4}{7} \times 360°$. Find the angle.

**g)** A coach travels 73 miles at an average speed of 33 mph. How long does it take?

**h)** Six friends share £14 between them. How much does each one get?

# EXERCISE 33.4H

**1** A boat travels 24 km in 3 hours. Calculate its average speed.

**2** A car covers 197 miles on a motorway in 3 hours. Calculate the average speed. Give your answer to 1 decimal place.

**3** Anne walks at an average speed of 3.5 km/h for 2 hours 30 minutes. How far does she walk?

**4** How long will it take a boat sailing at 12 km/h to travel 64 km?

**5** The density of a rock is 9.3 g/cm³. Its volume is 60 cm³. What is its mass?

**6** Calculate the density of a piece of metal with mass 300 g and volume 84 cm³. Give your answer to a suitable degree of accuracy.

**7** A man walks 10 km in 2 hours 15 minutes. What is his average speed in km/h? Give your answer to a suitable degree of accuracy.

**8** Calculate the mass of a stone of volume 46 cm³ and density 7.6 g/cm³.

**9** Copper has a density of 8.9 g/cm³. Calculate the volume of a block of copper of mass 38 g. Give your answer to a suitable degree of accuracy.

**10** What is the density of gas if a mass of 32 kg occupies a volume of 25 m³? Give your answer to a suitable degree of accuracy.

**11** A small town in America has a population of 235 and covers an area of 35 km². Find the population density (number of people per square kilometre) of the town.

**12** A coach left the coach station at 09:10 and travelled 72 km in 90 minutes, arriving at Carter castle.

**a)** Calculate its average speed.

The coach stopped at the castle for $3\frac{1}{2}$ hours and then travelled back at an average speed of 55 km/h.

**b)** At what time did it arrive back? Give your answer to the nearest minute.

# 34 → PERIMETER, AREA AND VOLUME

## EXERCISE 34.1H

1   Find the perimeter of each of these shapes.

a)

b)

c)

d)

e)

f)

2   A square has sides of length 3.7 m. What is its perimeter?

3   A rectangle has sides of length 4.3 cm and 5.7 cm. What is its perimeter?

4   The front of a calculator is a rectangle with sides of length 13.5 cm and 6.5 cm. What is its perimeter?

5   The top of a filing cabinet is a rectangle with sides of length 60 cm and 45 cm. What is its perimeter?

# EXERCISE 34.2H

Find the area of each of these shapes.
Give your answers in cm².

**1**

**2**

**3**

**4**

**5**

# EXERCISE 34.3H

**1** Find the area of each of these rectangles.
Take care to give the correct units in
the answer.

**a)**

**b)**

**c)**

**d)**

**e)**

**f)**

**g)**

**h)**

**2** A rectangle measures 5.3 cm by
2.6 cm. Find its area.

**3** A square has sides of length 3.6 cm.
Find its area.

**4** A rectangle has sides of length 3.25 cm and 0.95 cm. Find its area.

**5** A rectangular field measures 35 m by 16 m. Find its area.

**6** A desk top is a rectangle measuring 1.2 m by 0.8 m. Find its area.

**7** A drive is a rectangle measuring 6.5 m by 2.8 m.
**a)** Find the area of the drive.

To pave the drive it costs £32.50 per square metre.
**b)** How much does it cost to pave the drive?

**8** A rectangular window measures 1.5 m by 3.5 m.
**a)** Find the area of the window.

Glass costs £25 per square metre.
**b)** How much does the glass for the window cost?

**5**

**6**

**7**

**8**

**9**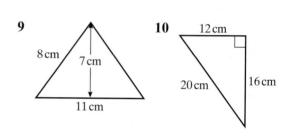

**10**

# EXERCISE 34.4H

Find the area of each of these triangles.

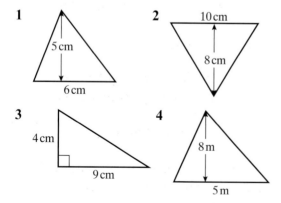

**1**

**2** 10 cm

8 cm

**3** 4 cm

9 cm

**4** 8 m

5 m

# EXERCISE 34.5H

Find the area of each of these parallelograms.

1
4 cm
7 cm

2
6 cm
9 cm

3
10 cm
2.5 cm

4
7 m
8 m

5
5 cm 6 cm
4 cm

6
4 cm
5.5 cm

7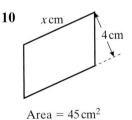
10 cm
5 cm
11 cm

8 
7 cm 6 cm
12 cm

Find the missing length in these diagrams.

9
h cm
5 cm
Area = 40 cm²

10
x cm
4 cm
Area = 45 cm²

# EXERCISE 34.6H

1 Find the volume of these cuboids.

a)
5 cm
2 cm
4 cm

b)
6 cm
3 cm
7 cm

2 A cuboid has a height of 6 cm, a length of 4 cm and a width of 5 cm.
Find its volume.

3 A cube has edges 4 cm long. Find its volume.

4 A cuboid has a square base with sides of length 4.5 cm and is 6 cm high.
Find its volume.

5 Calculate the volume of a cube with edges 12 m long.

6 A camera box has a rectangular base measuring 16 cm by 14 cm and is 12 cm high.
Calculate its volume.

7 A fish tank has a rectangular base measuring 15 cm by 60 cm and is 25 cm deep.
Find the volume of the tank.

8 A box of chocolates is a cuboid 12.5 cm long, 6 cm wide and 4.6 cm deep.
Calculate its volume.

**9** A biscuit tin is a cuboid 12 cm long,
4.5 cm wide and 6.5 cm deep.
Work out its volume.

**10** A piece of wood is a cuboid 3 m wide,
60 cm long and 2.5 cm thick.
Find the volume of the wood.
Hint: Be careful with the units.

# 35 → AREAS, VOLUMES AND 2-D REPRESENTATION

## EXERCISE 35.1H

Find the circumferences of circles with these diameters.

| | | |
|---|---|---|
| **1** 8 cm | **2** 17 cm | **3** 39.2 cm |
| **4** 116 mm | **5** 5.1 m | **6** 6.32 m |
| **7** 14 cm | **8** 23 cm | **9** 78 mm |
| **10** 39 mm | **11** 4.4 m | **12** 2.75 m |

## EXERCISE 35.2H

**1** Find the areas of circles with the following radii.

| | |
|---|---|
| **a)** 17 cm | **b)** 23 cm |
| **c)** 67 cm | **d)** 43 mm |
| **e)** 74 mm | **f)** 32 cm |
| **g)** 58 cm | **h)** 4.3 cm |
| **i)** 8.7 cm | **j)** 47 m |
| **k)** 1.9 m | **l)** 2.58 m |

**2** Find the areas of circles with the following diameters.

| | |
|---|---|
| **a)** 18 cm | **b)** 28 cm |
| **c)** 68 cm | **d)** 38 mm |
| **e)** 78 mm | **f)** 58 cm |
| **g)** 46 cm | **h)** 6.4 cm |
| **i)** 7.6 cm | **j)** 32 m |
| **k)** 3.4 m | **l)** 4.32 m |

## EXERCISE 35.3H

Find the area of each of these shapes. Break them down into rectangles and right-angled triangles first.

**1**

**2**

**3**

**4**

**5**

**6**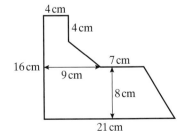

# EXERCISE 35.4H

Find the volume of each of these shapes.

**1**

**2**

**3**

**4**

**5**

**6**

# EXERCISE 35.5H

Find the volume of each of these prisms.

**1**

**2**

**3**

**4**

**5**

**6**

# EXERCISE 35.6H

Find the volumes of cylinders with these dimensions.

1 Radius 7 cm and height 29 cm
2 Radius 13 cm and height 27 cm
3 Radius 25 cm and height 80 cm
4 Radius 14 mm and height 35 mm
5 Radius 28 mm and height 8 mm
6 Radius 0.6 mm and height 5.1 mm
7 Radius 1.7 m and height 5 m
8 Radius 2.6 m and height 3.4 m

# EXERCISE 35.7H

1 Find the curved surface areas of cylinders with these dimensions.
   a) Radius 9 cm and height 16 cm
   b) Radius 13 cm and height 21 cm
   c) Radius 27 cm and height 12 cm
   d) Radius 17 mm and height 35 mm
   e) Radius 12 mm and height 6 mm
   f) Radius 3.7 mm and height 63 mm
   g) Radius 1.9 m and height 19 m
   h) Radius 2.7 m and height 4.3 m

2 Find the total surface areas of cylinders with these dimensions.
   a) Radius 8 cm and height 11 cm
   b) Radius 17 cm and height 28 cm
   c) Radius 29 cm and height 15 cm
   d) Radius 32 mm and height 8 mm
   e) Radius 35 mm and height 12 mm
   f) Radius 3.9 mm and height 45 mm
   g) Radius 0.8 m and height 7 m
   h) Radius 2.9 m and height 1.7 m

# EXERCISE 35.8H

Draw the plan view, front elevation and side elevation of each of these objects.

1

2

3

4

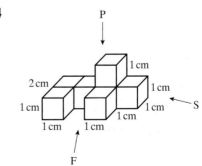

## EXERCISE 36.1H

For each of these diagrams, find the area of the third square.

**1**

**2**

**3**

**4**

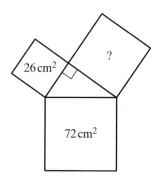

## EXERCISE 36.2H

**1** For each of these triangles, find the length marked $x$.
Where the answer is not exact, give your answer correct to 2 decimal places.

**a)**

**b)**

**c)**

**d)**

**e)**

**f)**

**g)**

**h)**

**2** Ann can walk home from school along two roads or along a path across a field.

How much shorter is her journey if she takes the path across the field?

**3** This network is made of wire.

What is the total length of wire?

**4** A tangent is drawn from a point P to meet the circle, centre O, at the point T such that TP = 12.8 cm and PȚO is a right angle. Given that the distance OP = 16.5 cm, calculate the radius of the circle.

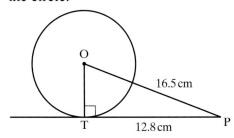

**5** A prism has a uniform cross-section in the shape of a triangle ABC, right angled at B and in which AC = 5.6 cm and AB = 3.4 cm. The length of the prism is 14.5 cm. Calculate the volume of the prism.

# EXERCISE 36.3H

Work out whether or not each of these triangles is right-angled.
Show your working.

**1**
15 cm  20 cm
25 cm

**2**
7.3 m  4.2 m
8.7 m

**3**
12 cm  12 cm
15 cm

**4**
40.3 cm
15.5 cm  37.2 cm

**5**
8 m
11 m
7 m

**6**
6.5 m
12.8 m  11.1 m

**7**
8.4 cm
30 cm
28.8 cm

**8**
30.2 cm
27.2 cm  13.5 cm

# EXERCISE 36.4H

1   Find the coordinates of the midpoint of
    each of the lines in the diagram.

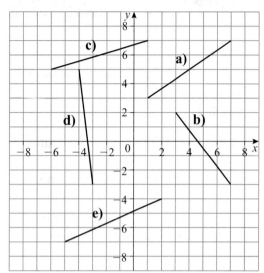

2   Find the coordinates of the midpoint of
    the line joining each of these pairs of
    points.
    Try to do them without plotting the
    points.
    a)  A(3, 7) and B(−5, 7)
    b)  C(2, 1) and D(8, 5)
    c)  E(3, 7) and F(8, 2)
    d)  G(1, 6) and H(9, 3)
    e)  I(−7, 1) and J(3, 6)
    f)  K(−5, −6) and L(−7, −3)

**EXERCISE 37.1H**

1  How many hours and minutes are there between these times?
   a)  08:10 and 08:43
   b)  15:00 and 19:00
   c)  10:42 and 11:23
   d)  13:48 and 15:22
   e)  06:41 and 14:25
   f)  22:10 on Thursday and 04:20 on Friday
   g)  $\frac{1}{4}$ to 4 and $\frac{1}{2}$ past 5
   h)  20 minutes to 5 and 25 minutes past 8

2  Felicity arrived at the dentist at 12:40. She was at the dentist for 35 minutes. At what time did she leave?

3  Gary went to town on a bus. He arrived at the bus stop at 09:55 and waited 8 minutes for the bus. The bus took 23 minutes to get to town. At what time did Gary arrive in town?

4  a)  On weekdays a train leaves Sheffield for London at 13:27 and arrives in London at 15:50. How long does the journey take?
   b)  On Sundays a train leaves Sheffield for London at 12:51. It takes 3 hours and 13 minutes. At what time does the train arrive in London?

5  James has an appointment for 10:15. He arrives 16 minutes early. At what time does he arrive?

6  At what time do these TV programmes finish?
   a)  Starts at 08:15 and lasts 30 minutes
   b)  Starts at 12:20 and lasts 50 minutes
   c)  Starts at 18:25 and lasts 40 minutes
   d)  Starts at 20:33 and lasts 1 hour 35 minutes
   e)  Starts at 22:35 on Tuesday and lasts 2 hours 20 minutes

7  Rupinder goes for lunch at 12:35 and returns at 13:47. For how long is she away?

8  Adam arrives 8 minutes early for a meeting due to start at 19:30. It starts 3 minutes late and finishes at 21:18.
   a)  At what time did Adam arrive?
   b)  How long was the meeting?

9  Rachel runs the 10 000 m race in 38 minutes 14 seconds. Caroline runs it in 39 minutes and 2 seconds. How much longer did it take Caroline?

10  Emily runs in a marathon. She checks the exact time that she crosses the start line. It is 10:41:05. She completes the race in a time of 4 hours 13 minutes and 6 seconds. What time is it when she finishes?

# EXERCISE 37.2H

1  Kieran drove 180 kilometres at an average speed of 40 km/h.
   How long did he take?

2  Imogen walked at an average speed of 5 km/h for 3 hours 30 minutes.
   How far did she walk?

3  Patrick drove 189 miles in $4\frac{1}{2}$ hours.
   What was his average speed in miles per hour?

4  A car travels at an average speed of 84 km/h.
   How far does it travel in 2.6 hours?

5  It took Peter 4 minutes 10 seconds to run 1000 metres.
   What was his speed in metres per second.

6  Mandy went on a ride on her motorbike. Her average speed was 96 km/h and she took 1 hour 40 minutes.
   How far did she travel?

7  A plane takes 3 hours 30 minutes to fly 2611 km.
   What is its average speed?

8  The distance from Lake Louise to Radium Springs is 240 miles.
   Taj travelled at an average speed of 54 mph.
   How long did it take him? Give your answer correct to the nearest minute.

9  A long cycle race covers 275 km. The winner took 14 hours 15 minutes.
   What was his average speed? Give your answer correct to 1 decimal place.

10  a)  How long does it take to travel 100 miles at an average speed of 70 mph?
    b)  How much time do you save by travelling 10 mph faster?
        Give your answers correct to the nearest minute.

# EXERCISE 37.3H

Use these approximate conversions for changing between imperial and metric units.

| Length | Weight |
|---|---|
| 8 km ≈ 5 miles | 1 kg ≈ 2 pounds (lb) |
| 1 m ≈ 40 inches | 25 g ≈ 1 ounce (oz) |
| 1 inch ≈ 2.5 cm | **Capacity** |
| 1 foot (ft) ≈ 30 cm | 4 litres ≈ 7 pints (pt) |

1  Petra went on a 12 km hike.
   How far was this in miles?

2  For a party Jasmine bought a 2 litre carton of full cream milk and four 2 litre bottles of semi-skimmed milk.
   How many pints of milk is that altogether?

3  Simon's rucksack has a mass of 32 pounds.
   How much is this in kilograms?

4  Fitz bought four lengths of wood, each 8 foot long.
   What was the total length in metres and centimetres?

5  At the swimming baths there is a 5-metre diving board.
   How high is this in feet and inches?

**6** The distance from Sheffield to Cambridge is 185 miles via the M1, but only 148 miles if you cut across to the A1.
How much further, in kilometres, is the journey via the M1?

**7** My car holds 10 gallons of petrol (1 gallon = 8 pints).
How many litres does it hold? Give your answer to the nearest litre.

**8** On a flight passengers are each allowed to have luggage weighing up to 20 kg.
Use the more accurate conversion 1 kg = 2.2 lbs to find how much they are each allowed in pounds.

# EXERCISE 37.4H

**1** On holiday in France, Jason made this table of approximate conversions between kilometres per hour (km/h) and miles per hour (mph).

| km/h | 40 | 50 | 60 | 70 | 80 | 90 | 100 | 110 | 120 |
|------|----|----|----|----|----|----|-----|-----|-----|
| mph  | 25 | 30 | 40 | 45 | 50 | 55 | 60  | 65  | 75  |

A more accurate conversion is mph = km/h × 0.625.
**a)** Jason saw a speed limit sign of 90 km/h.
What is the speed limit in mph
   **(i)** according to his table?
   **(ii)** using the more accurate conversion?

**b)** Some of the conversions in the table are exactly the same as using the accurate conversion. List them.

**2** Here is part of a Sunday timetable for trains from Sheffield and Chesterfield to London St Pancras.

| Sheffield | Chesterfield | London St Pancras |
|-----------|--------------|-------------------|
| 0853 | 0906 | 1219 |
| 0951 | 1007 | 1318 |
| 1102 | 1113 | 1418 |
| 1251 | 1303 | 1604 |
| 1353 | 1407 | 1706 |
| 1443 | 1456 | 1755 |
| 1601 | 1616 | 1914 |
| 1830 | 1843 | 2141 |

**a)** At what time does the 1102 from Sheffield arrive at London St Pancras?
**b)** At what time does the train arriving in London at 1755 leave Chesterfield?
**c)** Which of the trains in the list completes the journey from Sheffield to London in the shortest time?

**3**

| Distances are in miles | Birmingham | Bristol | Edinburgh | Glasgow | Liverpool | London | York |
|---|---|---|---|---|---|---|---|
| Birmingham | | 87 | 286 | 287 | 90 | 110 | 127 |
| Bristol | 87 | | 364 | 365 | 159 | 116 | 214 |
| Edinburgh | 286 | 364 | | 44 | 210 | 373 | 184 |
| Glasgow | 287 | 365 | 44 | | 212 | 392 | 207 |
| Liverpool | 90 | 159 | 210 | 212 | | 197 | 97 |
| London | 110 | 116 | 373 | 392 | 197 | | 196 |
| York | 127 | 214 | 184 | 207 | 97 | 196 | |

Use the above mileage chart to find
a)  the distance from **Bristol** to **London**.
b)  the **total length** of a journey from **Glasgow** to **Edinburgh** to **York**.

**4**  The following timetable shows the times of buses from Cefn Park to Church Road.
The buses then return from Church Road to Cefn Park.

| Cefn Park – Church Road – Cefn Park | | | Bus Timetable | |
|---|---|---|---|---|
| | Service numbers | | | |
| | **2901** | **2902** | **2903** | **2904** |
| **Cefn Park** | 0932 | 1045 | 1212 | 1435 |
| Kings Road | | 1051 | 1218 | 1441 |
| Saint Mary Street | | 1058 | 1225 | 1448 |
| Castle Hill | | 1104 | 1231 | 1454 |
| **Church Road** | 0952 | 1111 | 1238 | 1501 |
| Castle Hill | 0959 | 1118 | | 1508 |
| Saint Mary Street | 1007 | 1126 | | 1516 |
| Kings Road | 1015 | 1134 | | 1524 |
| **Cefn Park** | 1024 | 1143 | 1258 | 1533 |

a)  What time does service 2902 leave Cefn Park?
At what **times** does service 2904 arrive at Kings Road?
b)  How long does it take service 2903 to travel from Cefn Park to Church Road and
return to Cefn Park?

**5  a)**

| Distances are in miles | London | Cardiff | Fishguard | Liverpool | Shrewsbury |
|---|---|---|---|---|---|
| London | | 152 | 263 | 203 | 156 |
| Cardiff | 152 | | 127 | 198 | 110 |
| Fishguard | 263 | 127 | | 167 | 132 |
| Liverpool | 203 | 198 | 167 | | 68 |
| Shrewsbury | 156 | 110 | 132 | 68 | |

Use the above mileage chart to find
  (i)  the distance from **Liverpool** to **Cardiff**.
  (ii) the total length of the journey from **London** to **Cardiff** to **Fishguard**.
**b)**  The following table is a section of the rail timetable from Swansea to London.

| | | | |
|---|---|---|---|
| Swansea | 0700 | 1030 | 1330 |
| Neath | 0710 | 1040 | 1340 |
| Port Talbot | 0719 | 1049 | 1349 |
| Bridgend | 0730 | 1100 | 1400 |
| Cardiff | 0755 | 1125 | 1425 |
| Newport | 0815 | 1145 | 1445 |
| Bristol Parkway | 0840 | 1210 | 1510 |
| Reading | 0926 | 1301 | 1601 |
| London | 0956 | 1330 | 1630 |

  (i)  How long should it take the 0700 train from **Swansea** to get to **Port Talbot**?
  (ii) How long should it take the 1330 train from **Swansea** to travel from **Cardiff** to **Bristol Parkway**?

##  EXERCISE 38.1H

Work out these on your calculator without writing down the answers to the middle stages.

If the answers are not exact, give them correct to 2 decimal places.

1  $\dfrac{7.3 + 8.5}{5.7}$

2  $\dfrac{158 + 1027}{125}$

3  $\dfrac{6.7 + 19.5}{12.2 - 5.7}$

4  $\sqrt{128 - 34.6}$

5  $5.7 + \dfrac{1.89}{0.9}$

6  $(12.6 - 9.8)^2$

7  $\dfrac{8.9}{2.3 \times 5.6}$

8  $\dfrac{15.4}{2.3^2}$

9  $10.9 \times (7.2 - 5.8)$

10  $\dfrac{4.8 + 6.2}{5.2 \times 6.5}$

11  $\dfrac{7.1}{\sqrt{15.3 \times 0.6}}$

12  $\dfrac{3 - \sqrt{2.73} + 5.1}{4}$

## EXERCISE 38.2H

 Do not use your calculator for questions 1 to 4.

1  These calculations are all wrong. This can be spotted quickly without working them out.
   For each one, give a reason why it is wrong.
   a)  $15.3 \div -5.1 = 5$
   b)  $8.7 \times 1.6 = 5.4375$
   c)  $4.7 \times 300 = 9400$
   d)  $7.5^2 = 46.25$

2  These calculations are all wrong. This can be spotted quickly without working them out.
   For each one, give a reason why it is wrong.
   a)  $5.400 \div 9 = 60$
   b)  $-6.2 \times -0.5 = -93.1$
   c)  $\sqrt{0.4} = 0.2$
   d)  $8.5 \times 7.1 = 60.36$

3  Estimate the answers to each of these calculations. Show your working.
   a)  $93 \times 108$
   b)  $0.61^2$
   c)  $-19.6 + 5.2$

4  Estimate the answers to these calculations. Show your working.
   a)  The cost of three DVDs at £17.99
   b)  The cost of 39 cinema tickets at £6.20
   c)  The cost of five meals at £7.99 and two drinks at £2.10

You may use your calculator for questions 5 to 9.

5  Use inverse operations to check these calculations. Write down the operations you use.
   a)  $19\,669.5 \div 235 = 83.7$
   b)  $\sqrt{5069.44} = 71.2$
   c)  $9.7 \times 12.4 = 120.28$
   d)  $17.2 \times 4.6 + 68.2 = 147.32$

**6** Work these out. Round your answers to 2 decimal places.

a) $\dfrac{24.3 + 18.6}{2.8 \times 0.51}$

b) $(13.7 + 53.1) \times (9.87 - 5.9)$

**7** Work these out. Round your answers to 3 decimal places.

a) $\dfrac{77.8}{6.4 + 83.9}$

b) $1.06^4 \times 185$

**8** Work these out. Round your answers to 2 significant figures.

a) $\sqrt{2.5^2 + 9.0}$

b) $640 \times 0.078$

**9** a) Use rounding to 1 significant figure to estimate the answer to each of these calculations. Show your working.

(i) $21.2^3$

(ii) $189 \times 0.31$

(iii) $\sqrt{11.1^2 - 4.8^2}$

(iv) $\dfrac{51.8 + 39.2}{0.022}$

b) Use your calculator to find the correct answer to each of the calculations in part **a)**. Where appropriate, round your answer to a sensible degree of accuracy.

# EXERCISE 38.3H

**1** Write each of these times as a decimal.

a) 8 hours 39 minutes

b) 5 hours 21 minutes

c) 33 minutes

d) 3 minutes

**2** Write each of these times in hours and minutes.

a) 4.8 hours      b) 5.85 hours

c) 0.45 hours      d) 0.6 hours

**3** a) A walker covers a distance of 7.2 miles in 2 hours and 24 minutes.
Calculate the average speed of the walker in miles per hour.

b) For one 25-minute section of its journey, an express train travels at an average speed of 126 miles per hour.
How long is this section of the journey? Give your answer in miles.

c) In one stage of its flight, a rocket travelled at a constant speed of 357 miles per hour for a distance of 23.8 miles.
How long did it take the rocket to travel that distance?

**4** In a four-part endurance race, a driver takes the following times to complete each part of the race.

5 hours 38 minutes
6 hours 57 minutes
5 hours 19 minutes
5 hours 46 minutes

What was the driver's total time for the race? Give your answer in hours and minutes.

**5** Wayne buys some potatoes at £1.25 a kilogram and six nectarines at 37p each.
He gives the shop assistant £10 and gets £4.68 change.
What weight of potatoes did he buy?

6  Chelsea, Sally and James share the profits from their business in the ratio 4 : 3 : 2.
In 2009 the total profit was £94 500.
Calculate how much Sally received.

7  Merry followed a recipe for lemon pudding which used 350 g of flour for four people.
He made the recipe for 10 people and used a new 1.5 kg bag of flour.
How much flour did he have left?

8  Freeville has a population of 36 281 and its area is 27.4 km².
Calculate its population density. Give your answer to a sensible degree of accuracy.

9  Mr Brown's mobile phone bill for March showed that he had used 53 minutes of calls at 13p per minute.
His monthly rental charge for the phone was £15.30.
There was VAT at 12.5% on the whole bill.
Calculate the total bill including VAT.

10  In January 2009, the Retail Price Index (RPI) was 210.1.
In January 2010 it was 217.9.
Calculate the percentage increase in the RPI over that year.

11  A metal cylinder has radius 3.8 cm and height 5.7 cm.
Its density is 12 g/cm³.
Calculate its mass.

12  A water urn is in the shape of a cuboid, with the base a square of side 30 cm.
How many litres of water does the urn contain when it is filled to a depth of 42 cm?

13  David drove 28 miles along the motorway at 70 mph, and then 10 miles at 50 mph.
    a)  Calculate how long he took.
    b)  Find his average speed for the whole journey.

# EXERCISE 39.1H

1  Choose the best probability word from those below to complete these sentences.

> impossible   unlikely      evens
> likely        certain

a) It is ..................... that the next baby born in Devon will be a boy.
b) It is ..................... that there will be snow at the South Pole next week.
c) It is ..................... that you will get more than 1 when you throw an ordinary dice.

2  Copy this scale.

> Impossible Unlikely  Evens    Likely   Certain

Put arrows to show the chance of each of the following events happening.
a) Water will come out when you turn on the tap.
b) It will be dark tonight.
c) Christmas Day falls on a Sunday.

3  There are 20 marbles in a tin. There are 3 red marbles, 10 green marbles and 7 yellow marbles.
A marble is taken out without looking. Choose the correct probability word to complete these sentences.
a) It is ..................... that the marble is red.

b) It is ..................... that the marble is blue.
c) It is ..................... that the marble is green.

# EXERCISE 39.2H

1  These six cards are laid face down and mixed up. Then a card is picked at random.

Copy this probability scale.

> Impossible                          Certain
> 0               0.5                  1

Put arrows to show the probability of each of the following events happening. The number on the card is
a) 3.
b) less than 6.
c) an even number.

2  There are ten pens in a bag.
Two are red, seven are blue and one is black.
A pen is taken out without looking.
a) Use a probability word to complete this sentence.

> It is ..................... that the pen is blue.

**b)** Copy this probability scale.

0    0.2    0.4    0.6    0.8    1.0

Mark the probability of each of these statements on your scale. Use arrows and label them R, G and B.
R: the pen is red.
G: the pen is green.
B: the pen is blue.

**3** This spinner is fair.

Calculate the probability of it landing on
**a)** 3.
**b)** an even number.
**c)** 4.

**4** An ordinary dice is thrown.
Find the probability of getting
**a)** an odd number.
**b)** a 4.

**5** Mary has ten pens. Three are black, five are blue and two are green.
She takes a pen without looking.
Giving your answer as a decimal, calculate the probability that the pen is
**a)** blue.
**b)** green.
**c)** not black.

**6** There are 12 counters in a bag. The probability scale shows the probabilities of choosing the different colours of counter.

How many counters of each colour are there in the bag?

**7** Gill has eight sweets in a bag. Three of them are yellow and the other five are pink.
**a)** She takes a sweet without looking. Which colour is she more likely to get?
**b)** Gill takes some sweets out of the bag.
There is now an even chance of getting a pink sweet.
How many sweets of each colour has she taken?

**8** Jack has ten pairs of socks. Three of these pairs are black.
He takes a pair of socks out of his drawer without looking.
Draw a probability scale numbered 0 to 1, like the one in question **2 b)**.
Mark the probability of each of these statements on your scale.
**a)** The socks are black.
**b)** The socks are not black.

**9** The probability is $\frac{3}{8}$ that when three coins are tossed, you get two heads and a tail.
What is the probability that you don't get two heads and a tail?

**10** There are five yellow counters, two red counters and eight black counters in a bag.
A counter is taken without looking. What is the probability that it is
**a)** yellow?
**b)** red?
**c)** not red?

## EXERCISE 39.3H

**1** Irina surveyed the favourite crisp flavour of people in her class.
Here are her results.

| Flavour | Frequency |
|---|---|
| Plain | 7 |
| Chicken | 5 |
| Cheese and Onion | 12 |
| BBQ | 2 |
| Other | 4 |

Calculate an estimate of the probability that the next person she asks will like cheese and onion best.

**2** Tim tests a spinner he has made to check it is fair.
He spins it 500 times.
Here are his results.

| Number on spinner | Frequency |
|---|---|
| 1 | 58 |
| 2 | 73 |
| 3 | 103 |
| 4 | 124 |
| 5 | 142 |

**a)** For this spinner, calculate the experimental probability of obtaining
**(i)** a 5. **(ii)** a 1.
**b)** For a fair spinner, calculate, as a decimal, the probability of scoring
**(i)** a 5. **(ii)** a 1.
**c)** Do your answers suggest that the spinner is fair? Give your reasons.

## REVIEW EXERCISE 39H

**1** A red bag contains five balls numbered as shown.

① ② ④ ⑥ ⑦

A blue bag contains six balls numbered as shown

① ③ ④ ⑥ ⑦ ⑧

In a game a player chooses a ball from the red bag and then a ball from the blue bag. The numbers on the two balls are added together to obtain a total score.

**a)** Copy and complete the following table to show all the possible total scores.

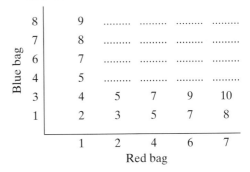

**b) (i)** What is the probability that a player gets a total score of 14?

**(ii)** What is the probability that a player does not get a total score of 14?

A player wins a prize by getting a total score of 5 or less.

**c) (i)** Tim plays the game once. What is the probability that he wins a prize?

**(ii)** 150 people each play the game once. Approximately how many would you expect to win a prize?

**(iii)** It costs 20p to play the game once. The prize for scoring 5 or less is 40p. If the 150 people each play the game once, approximately how much profit do you expect the game to make?

**2** A square shaped spinner has the numbers 0, 1, 2 and 3 written on it. Another spinner, in the shape of a regular pentagon, has the numbers 1, 2, 3, 4 and 5 written on it.

In a game, a player spins both spinners and multiplies the two numbers showing on the spinners to get the score for the game.

For example, if the number on the square spinner is 3 and the number on the pentagon spinner is 2, the player works out $3 \times 2 = 6$ and the player scores 6.

**a)** Copy and complete the following table to show all the possible scores.

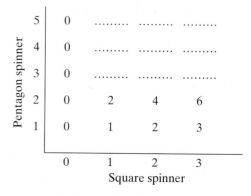

| Pentagon spinner | | Square spinner | | |
|---|---|---|---|---|
| 5 | 0 | ......... | ......... | ......... |
| 4 | 0 | ......... | ......... | ......... |
| 3 | 0 | ......... | ......... | ......... |
| 2 | 0 | 2 | 4 | 6 |
| 1 | 0 | 1 | 2 | 3 |
| | 0 | 1 | 2 | 3 |

**b) (i)** What is the probability that a player scores 0?

**(ii)** What is the probability that a player does not score 0?

A player wins a prize by getting a score of 2 or less.

**c)** Barbara plays the game once. What is the probability that she wins a prize?

**d) (i)** 600 people each play the game once. Approximately how many would you expect to win a prize?

**(ii)** It costs 30p to play the game once. The prize for getting a score of 2 or less is 50p. If the 600 people each play the game once, approximately how much profit do you expect the game to make?

**3** Jane throws a fair dice. On a copy of the scale given below mark the points A, B and C where

A is the probability that the score will be a 5.

B is the probability that the score will be an even number.

C is the probability that the score will be an 8.

```
├──────────────┼──────────────┤
0                              1
```

**4** In a game, a player throws two fair dice, one coloured red the other blue.

The score for the throw is the smaller of the numbers showing. For example, if the red dice shows 5 and the blue dice shows 2, the score for the throw is 2; if the red dice shows 3 and the blue dice shows 3, the score for the throw is 3.

**a)** Copy and complete the following table to show all the possible scores.

| Red dice | | | | | | |
|---|---|---|---|---|---|---|
| 6 | 1 | 2 | 3 | ........ | ........ | ........ |
| 5 | 1 | 2 | 3 | ........ | ........ | ........ |
| 4 | 1 | 2 | 3 | ........ | ........ | ........ |
| 3 | 1 | 2 | 3 | 3 | ........ | ........ |
| 2 | 1 | 2 | 2 | 2 | ........ | ........ |
| 1 | 1 | 1 | 1 | 1 | 1 | 1 |
| | 1 | 2 | 3 | 4 | 5 | 6 |

Blue dice

**b)** **(i)** What is the probability that a player scores 1?

**(ii)** What is the probability that a player scores more than 1?

A player wins a prize by getting a score of 2 or less.

**c)** William plays the game once. What is the probability that he wins a prize?

**d)** **(i)** 360 people each play the game once. Approximately how many would you expect to win a prize?

**(ii)** It costs £1 to play the game once. The prize for winning is £1.50. If the 360 people each play the game once, approximately how much profit do you expect the game to make?

**5** **a)** Using a copy of the probability scale below mark the points A, B and C where

A is the probability that there will be snow at the north pole in January.

B is the probability that it will rain in the Sahara desert tomorrow.

C is the probability that the score will be a 2 when an ordinary dice is rolled.

```
├──────────────┼──────────────┤
0             0.5             1
```

**b)** One-hundred-and-fifty-five children in a school each buy one raffle ticket.

Wyn buys one of the raffle tickets.

**(i)** What is the probability of Wyn winning the raffle?

**(ii)** Wyn believes that the probability of the raffle being won by a boy is $\frac{1}{2}$. Is Wyn correct? Give a reason for your answer.

**6**

Tim has six cards with shapes on them, as shown above.

a) Tim chooses one card at random. Draw the shape he is most likely to choose.

b) On a copy of the probability scale shown below, mark the points A, B and C where

A is the probability of Tim choosing a ♠

B is the probability of Tim choosing a ♦

C is the probability of Tim choosing a ♥

```
 +———————————————+———————————————
 0               |               1
```

## EXERCISE 40.1H

1   The probability that Stacey will go to bed late tonight is 0.2.
What is the probability that Stacey will not go to bed late tonight?

2   The probability that I will throw a six with a dice is $\frac{1}{6}$.
What is the probability that I will not throw a six?

3   The probability that it will snow on Christmas Day is 0.15.
What is the probability that it will not snow on Christmas Day?

4   The probability that someone chosen at random is left-handed is $\frac{3}{10}$.
What is the probability that someone chosen at random will be right-handed?

5   The probability that United will lose their next game is 0.08.
What is the probability that United will not lose their next game?

6   The probability that Ian will eat crisps tomorrow is $\frac{17}{31}$.
What is the probability that he will not eat crisps tomorrow?

## EXERCISE 40.2H

1   A shop has brown, white and wholemeal bread for sale.
The probability that someone will choose brown bread is 0.4 and the probability that they will choose white bread is 0.5.
What is the probability of someone choosing wholemeal bread?

2   A football coach is choosing a striker for the next game.
He has three players to choose from; Wayne, Michael and Alan.
The probability that he will choose Wayne is $\frac{5}{19}$ and the probability that he will choose Michael is $\frac{7}{19}$.
What is the probability that he will choose Alan?

3   A bag contains red, white and blue counters. Jill chooses a counter at random.
The probability that she chooses a red counter is 0.4 and the probability that she chooses a blue counter is 0.15.
What is the probability that she chooses a white counter?

4   Elaine goes to town by car, bus, taxi or bike.
    The probability that she uses her car is $\frac{12}{31}$, the probability that she catches the bus is $\frac{2}{31}$ and the probability that she takes a taxi is $\frac{13}{31}$.
    What is the probability that she rides her bike into town?

5   A biased five-sided spinner is numbered 1 to 5. The table shows the probability of obtaining some of the scores when it is spun.

| Score | 1 | 2 | 3 | 4 | 5 |
|---|---|---|---|---|---|
| Probability | 0.37 | 0.1 | 0.14 | | 0.22 |

What is the probability of getting 4?

6   A cash bag contains only £20, £10 and £5 notes. One note is chosen from the bag at random.
    There is a probability of $\frac{3}{4}$ that it is a £5 note and a probability of $\frac{3}{20}$ that it is a £10 note.
    What is the probability that it is a £20 note?

# EXERCISE 40.3H

1   The probability that United will lose a game is 0.2.
    How many games would you expect them to lose in a season of 40 games?

2   The probability that it will be rainy on any day in June is $\frac{2}{15}$.
    On how many of June's 30 days would you expect it to be rainy?

3   The probability that an eighteen-year-old driver will have an accident is 0.15. There are 80 eighteen-year-old drivers in a school.
    How many of them might be expected to have an accident?

4   When Phil is playing chess, the probability that he wins is $\frac{17}{20}$.
    In a competition, Phil plays 10 games. How many of them might you expect him to win?

5   An ordinary six-sided dice is thrown 90 times. How many times might you expect to get
    a)  a 4?           b)  an odd number?

6   A box contains twelve yellow balls, three blue balls and five green balls. A ball is chosen at random and its colour noted.
    The ball is then replaced. This is done 400 times.
    How many of each colour might you expect to get?

# EXERCISE 40.4H

1   Pete rolls a dice 200 times and records the number of times each score appears.

| Score | 1 | 2 | 3 | 4 | 5 | 6 |
|---|---|---|---|---|---|---|
| Frequency | 29 | 34 | 35 | 32 | 34 | 36 |

a)  Work out the relative frequency of each of the scores.
    Give your answers to 2 decimal places.
b)  Do you think that Pete's dice is fair? Give a reason for your answer.

**2**  Rory kept a record of his favourite football team's results.

   Win: 32    Draw: 11    Lose: 7

   a) Calculate the relative frequency of each of the three outcomes.
   b) Are your answers to part **a)** good estimates of the probability of the outcome of their next match? Give a reason for your answer.

**3**  In a survey, 600 people were asked which flavour of crisps they preferred. The results are shown in the table.

| Flavour | Frequency |
|---|---|
| Plain | 166 |
| Salt & Vinegar | 130 |
| Cheese & Onion | 228 |
| Other | 76 |

   a) Work out the relative frequency of each flavour. Give your answers to 2 decimal places.
   b) Explain why it is reasonable to use these figures to estimate the probability of the flavour of crisps that the next person to be asked will prefer.

**4**  The owner of a petrol station notices that, in one day, 287 out of 340 people filling their car with petrol spent over £20.
   Use these figures to estimate the probability that the next customer will spend
   a) over £20.        b) £20 or less.

**5**  Jasmine made a spinner numbered 1, 2, 3, 4 and 5.
   She tested the spinner to see if it was fair.
   The results are shown below.

| Score | 1 | 2 | 3 | 4 | 5 |
|---|---|---|---|---|---|
| Frequency | 46 | 108 | 203 | 197 | 96 |

   a) Work out the relative frequency of each of the scores. Give your answers to 2 decimal places.
   b) Do you think that the spinner is fair? Give a reason for your answer.

**6**  A box contains yellow, green, white and blue counters.
   A counter is chosen from the box and its colour noted. The counter is then replaced in the box.
   The table below gives information about the colour of counter picked.

| Colour | Relative frequency |
|---|---|
| Yellow | 0.4 |
| Green | 0.3 |
| White | 0.225 |
| Blue | 0.075 |

   a) There are 80 counters altogether in the box.
      How many do you think there are of each colour?
   b) What other information is needed before you can be sure that your answers to part **a)** are accurate?

## EXERCISE 41.1H

1   Which of the following are discrete
data and which are continuous data?

Time of day
Weight of an egg
Number of peas in a pod
Day you were born
Amount of rain in a week
Price of an item

2   List at least three more examples of
a)   continuous data.
b)   discrete data.

3   Design a data collection sheet for each
of the following.
a)   Favourite school subject
b)   Favourite sport
c)   School shoe colour

## EXERCISE 41.2H

1   Draw a vertical line graph to show
each of these sets of data.

a)

| Type of fast food | Frequency |
|---|---|
| Pizza | 18 |
| Chinese | 8 |
| Burger | 13 |
| Kebab | 6 |
| Fish and chips | 4 |
| Other | 25 |

b)

| Type of vehicle | Frequency |
|---|---|
| Car | 43 |
| Van | 29 |
| Lorry | 15 |
| Bus | 7 |
| Motorbike | 4 |
| Other | 2 |

c)

| Type of tree | Frequency |
|---|---|
| Oak | 3 |
| Beech | 7 |
| Pine | 10 |
| Sycamore | 6 |
| Lime | 2 |
| Other | 2 |

2   Draw a bar chart to show each of these
sets of data.

a)

| Favourite colour | Frequency |
|---|---|
| Blue | 23 |
| Red | 9 |
| Green | 6 |
| Yellow | 4 |
| Pink | 7 |
| Black | 3 |
| Other | 8 |

**b)**

| Number of sisters | Frequency |
|---|---|
| 0 | 7 |
| 1 | 12 |
| 2 | 8 |
| 3 | 2 |
| 4 or more | 1 |

**c)**

| Shoe size | Frequency |
|---|---|
| 39 | 12 |
| 40 | 8 |
| 41 | 15 |
| 42 | 11 |
| 43 | 9 |
| 44 | 6 |
| 45 | 2 |
| Other | 7 |

**d)**

| Type of bird | Frequency |
|---|---|
| Sparrow | 41 |
| Starling | 32 |
| Pigeon | 14 |
| Finch | 5 |
| Dove | 2 |
| Other | 6 |

**e)**

| Drinks per day | Frequency |
|---|---|
| Less than 4 | 5 |
| 4 | 12 |
| 5 | 21 |
| 6 | 28 |
| 7 | 23 |
| 8 or more | 11 |

**f)**

| Number of pets | Frequency |
|---|---|
| 0 | 14 |
| 1 | 45 |
| 2 | 23 |
| 3 | 12 |
| 4 | 5 |
| 5 or more | 1 |

3   Sally does a survey to find out what pupils think of school lunch. Her results are shown in the following table.

| Satisfaction level | Replies | Frequency |
|---|---|---|
| Excellent | ||||| ||||| ||||| ||||| ||||| || | |
| Good | ||||| ||||| ||||| ||| | |
| Fair | ||||| ||||| ||||| | | |
| Poor | ||||| ||||| ||||| ||||| || | |

Copy and complete the frequency column in the above table and use this data to draw a suitable bar chart.

4   Ann carried out a survey of the colour of cars parked at a hotel near her home. She recorded the colours in the following way.

**R – red          B – blue      G – green**
**W – white        S – silver**
**O – other colours**

The results of her survey are as follows.

**R  R  B  W  W  S  O  O  O  R  S**
**S  S  W  G  G  R  R  B  S  S  O**
**O  W  R  S  S  G  B  G  B  W  O**
**S  S  R  R  W  R  S  G  G  S  W**

**a)** Using the above data copy and complete the following table.

| Colour | Replies | Frequency |
|---|---|---|
| Red | ~~IIII~~ IIII | 9 |
| Blue | | |
| Green | | |
| White | | |
| Silver | | |
| Other colours | | |

**b)** Use this data to draw a suitable bar chart.

**5** Tom carries out a survey, in his class, to find the colour of pupils' eyes. His results are shown in the following table.

| Colour | Number of pupils | Frequency |
|---|---|---|
| Blue | ~~IIII~~ ~~IIII~~ III | |
| Green | ~~IIII~~ II | |
| Brown | ~~IIII~~ ~~IIII~~ ~~IIII~~ | |

Copy and complete the frequency column in the above table and use this data to draw a suitable bar chart.

# EXERCISE 41.3H

**1** Here is a two-way table showing the results of a car survey.
Copy and complete the table.

| | Black | Not black | Total |
|---|---|---|---|
| German | 18 | 49 | |
| Not German | 23 | 64 | |
| Total | | | |

**2** Here is a two-way table showing the results of a survey of vehicles in a car park.

**a)** Copy and complete the table.

| | White | Not white | Total |
|---|---|---|---|
| Car | 3 | 86 | |
| Not car | 24 | 7 | |
| Total | | | |

**b)** How many white cars were in the survey?
**c)** How many cars were in the survey?
**d)** How many vehicles were not white?
**e)** How many vehicles were surveyed in total?

**3** Here is a two-way table showing the sales made by a bookshop on one day.

**a)** Copy and complete the table.

|  | Paperback | Not paperback | Total |
|---|---|---|---|
| **Fiction** |  | 11 | 98 |
| **Non-fiction** | 9 | 17 |  |
| **Total** |  |  |  |

**b)** How many non-fiction books were sold?

**c)** How many paperback fiction books were sold?

**d)** How many books were sold in total?

**4** A group of students were questioned about their favourite subject and their preferred writing hand.
Here is a two-way table showing the results.

**a)** Copy and complete the table.

|  | Right hand | Left hand | Neither | Total |
|---|---|---|---|---|
| **Maths** | 27 | 8 | 1 |  |
| **Not maths** |  | 13 |  | 112 |
| **Total** | 126 |  |  |  |

**b)** How many students were left-handed?

**c)** How many students chose maths?

**d)** How many right-handed students chose a subject other than maths?

**e)** How many students were in the survey?

**5** At a swimming championship, Australia, China and the USA won most medals. Their results are shown in the table.

**a)** Copy and complete the table.

|  | Gold | Silver | Bronze | Total |
|---|---|---|---|---|
| **Australia** |  | 27 | 13 | 74 |
| **China** |  | 20 |  | 63 |
| **USA** | 21 | 19 |  | 59 |
| **Total** | 71 |  |  |  |

**b)** How many silver medals were awarded in total to these countries?

**c)** How many gold medals did Australia win?

**d)** Which of these countries won most bronze medals?

**e)** How many medals were awarded in total to these countries?

# EXERCISE 41.4H

**1** Draw a frequency table using tallies for each of these sets of data.

**a)** Marks out of 30 in a maths test
Use groups of 1 to 5, 6 to 10, 11 to 15, 16 to 20, ... .

| 14 | 26 | 16 | 24 | 13 | 4 | 8 | 22 | 20 | 24 |
|---|---|---|---|---|---|---|---|---|---|
| 2 | 25 | 15 | 16 | 22 | 11 | 10 | 23 | 8 | 23 |
| 23 | 17 | 5 | 7 | 17 | 9 | 12 | 18 | 17 | 18 |
| 7 | 29 | 8 | 18 | 14 | 16 | 13 | 16 | 6 | 6 |
| 13 | 16 | 14 | 9 | 6 | 19 | 7 | 13 | 15 | 4 |
| 19 | 21 | 19 | 14 | 9 | 3 | 7 | 23 | 19 | 21 |

**b)** Number of apples on a tree
Use groups of 1 to 10, 11 to 20, 21 to 30, ... .

| 43 | 34 | 17 | 37 | 18 | 42 | 11 | 37 | 18 | 15 |
|---|---|---|---|---|---|---|---|---|---|
| 24 | 25 | 23 | 23 | 30 | 24 | 13 | 16 | 28 | 21 |
| 15 | 37 | 35 | 27 | 28 | 33 | 21 | 27 | 6 | 18 |
| 23 | 2 | 29 | 39 | 31 | 40 | 36 | 86 | 27 | 46 |
| 7 | 25 | 21 | 19 | 90 | 29 | 27 | 24 | 14 | 27 |
| 36 | 21 | 30 | 25 | 22 | 31 | 29 | 37 | 7 | 43 |

**c)** Number of lorries delivering to a depot per day
Use groups of 0 to 19, 20 to 39, 40 to 59, ... .

```
49  41  63  36  29  53  65  46  27  48
51  74  52  44  47  77  87  35  69  74
53  27  44  50  67   9  36  14  31  42
73  55  35  53  83  45  62  53  43  61
 4  62  28  37  16  43  45  32  55  43
66  37  17  18  33  38  57  51  77  66
```

**2** Draw a bar chart for each of these sets of data.

**a)**

| Number of video games | Frequency |
|---|---|
| 1 to 5 | 7 |
| 6 to 10 | 14 |
| 11 to 15 | 31 |
| 16 to 20 | 27 |
| 21 to 25 | 11 |
| 26 or more | 10 |

**b)**

| Number of swimmers | Frequency |
|---|---|
| 0 to 49 | 2 |
| 50 to 99 | 5 |
| 100 to 149 | 11 |
| 150 to 199 | 9 |
| 200 to 249 | 3 |
| 250 or more | 1 |

**c)**

| Number of eggs | Frequency |
|---|---|
| 1 to 5 | 5 |
| 6 to 10 | 8 |
| 11 to 15 | 17 |
| 16 to 20 | 23 |
| 21 to 25 | 9 |
| 26 or more | 3 |

**d)**

| Number of runners | Frequency |
|---|---|
| 1 to 5 | 9 |
| 6 to 10 | 17 |
| 11 to 15 | 18 |
| 16 to 20 | 4 |
| 21 or more | 2 |

**e)**

| Number of balloons | Frequency |
|---|---|
| 0 to 9 | 4 |
| 10 to 19 | 11 |
| 20 to 29 | 27 |
| 30 to 39 | 35 |
| 40 to 49 | 21 |
| 50 to 59 | 13 |
| 60 to 69 | 5 |
| 70 or more | 9 |

**f)**

| Number of fish | Frequency |
|---|---|
| 1 to 10 | 9 |
| 11 to 20 | 9 |
| 21 to 30 | 15 |
| 31 to 40 | 28 |
| 41 to 50 | 7 |
| 51 or more | 2 |

## EXERCISE 42.1H

1   The numbers of cars of different colours passing a school one lunchtime were as follows.

Black    15
Blue     25
Green    10
Red      20
Silver   30
Other    35

Draw a pictogram to show this data using ● to represent 10 cars.

2   The numbers of fish caught each day one week in a fishing lake were as follows.

Monday      12
Tuesday     8
Wednesday   10
Thursday    4
Friday      9
Saturday    18
Sunday      27

Draw a pictogram to show this data using ■ to represent four fish.

3   The numbers of people taking an early morning swim each day one week at a leisure centre were as follows.

Monday      16
Tuesday     14
Wednesday   18
Thursday    15
Friday      16
Saturday    10
Sunday      8

Create your own symbol for four swimmers and draw a pictogram to show this data.

4   The numbers of umbrellas sold each month one year by a department store were as follows.

January     40
February    20
March       60
April       80
May         50
June        30
July        15
August      10
September   25
October     55
November    40
December    65

Draw a pictogram to show this data.

# EXERCISE 42.2H

1  Draw a pie chart for each of these sets of data.

a)

| Favourite drink | Frequency |
|---|---|
| Soft drink | 42 |
| Milk | 12 |
| Water | 48 |
| Juice | 18 |
| Other | 60 |
| Total | 180 |

b)

| Eye colour | Frequency |
|---|---|
| Blue | 76 |
| Green | 28 |
| Brown | 92 |
| Grey | 38 |
| Other | 6 |
| Total | 240 |

c)

| Type of programme | Frequency |
|---|---|
| Comedy | 14 |
| Soap | 22 |
| Cartoon | 16 |
| Drama | 18 |
| Other | 10 |
| Total | 80 |

2  Draw a pie chart for each of these sets of data.

a)

| Activity | Hours |
|---|---|
| School | 6 |
| Sleeping | 9 |
| Eating | 2 |
| Playing | 3 |
| TV | 2 |
| Other | 2 |

b)

| Favourite TV channel | Frequency |
|---|---|
| BBC | 12 |
| ITV | 15 |
| Channel 4 | 6 |
| Five | 9 |
| Satellite/Cable | 30 |

c)

| Favourite type of film | Frequency |
|---|---|
| Comedy | 25 |
| Horror | 14 |
| Romance | 32 |
| Action | 17 |
| Other | 2 |

# EXERCISE 42.3H

1   The table shows the maximum daytime temperature in Miami over a period of 12 days.

| Day | Mon | Tues | Wed | Thur | Fri | Sat | Sun | Mon | Tues | Wed | Thur | Fri |
|---|---|---|---|---|---|---|---|---|---|---|---|---|
| Temp. (°C) | 27 | 29 | 28 | 31 | 33 | 34 | 37 | 36 | 33 | 32 | 30 | 31 |

Draw a line graph to show this information.

2   The table shows the monthly sales of gravel by a garden centre in 2009.

| Month | Jan | Feb | Mar | Apr | May | June | July | Aug | Sept | Oct | Nov | Dec |
|---|---|---|---|---|---|---|---|---|---|---|---|---|
| Sales (tonnes) | 2 | 3 | 5 | 8 | 13 | 11 | 6 | 5 | 7 | 8 | 4 | 1 |

Draw a line graph to show this information.

3   The table shows the number of tickets sold by a cinema one week.

| Day | Mon | Tues | Wed | Thur | Fri | Sat | Sun |
|---|---|---|---|---|---|---|---|
| Tickets | 58 | 71 | 49 | 86 | 183 | 205 | 152 |

Draw a line graph to show this information.

4   The table shows the monthly sales of widgets in 2009.

| Month | Jan | Feb | Mar | Apr | May | June | July | Aug | Sept | Oct | Nov | Dec |
|---|---|---|---|---|---|---|---|---|---|---|---|---|
| Sales (×£1000) | 3 | 5 | 8 | 13 | 24 | 36 | 29 | 18 | 13 | 9 | 6 | 4 |

Draw a line graph to show this information.

# 43 → MEASURES OF AVERAGE AND SPREAD

## EXERCISE 43.1H

1   Find the median of each of these sets of data.
    a)  1   4   5   7   9   9   10
    b)  3   9   6   4   3   9   3   2   7
    c)  4   5   9   6   9   9   7   4   8   8
    d)  2   5   3   2   7   8   9   3   4
    e)  3   7   1   3   5   7   9   11

2   Find the median of these seven weekly wages.
    £257   £238   £289   £362
    £321   £411   £306

3   The ages of six teachers are as follows.
    46   52   38   25   31   62
    Find the median age.

4   These are Sophie's marks in five tests.
    5   8   9   7   8
    These are Carole's marks in six tests.
    7   6   9   4   8   3
    a)  Find the median mark for
        (i) Sophie.      (ii) Carole.
    b)  Who had the higher median mark?

5   Stephen is asked to find the median of these numbers.
    4   2   1   5   7
    He says the median is 1. He is wrong.
    a)  What has he done wrong?
    b)  What is the correct answer?

## EXERCISE 43.2H

1   Find the mode of this set of data.
    1   2   1   3   2   4
    3   5   2   5   2

2   The number of boys who were at ten different sports practices were as follows.
    18   17   17   20   16
    20   9   9   17   10
    Find the modal number of boys at a practice.

3   The marks scored in a test were as follows.
    10   12   18   17   16   18   14   15
    16   18   14   18   20   9   18   13
    Find the modal number of marks scored.

4   Here is a list of the heights of ten people.
    173 cm   158 cm   161 cm   163 cm
    181 cm   153 cm   173 cm   170 cm
    162 cm   180 cm
    Find the modal height.

5   The ages of a group of friends are as follows.
    18   22   21   19   18
    18   17   19   17   21
    Find the modal age.

# EXERCISE 43.3H

1   Find the mean of this set of data.

   3   6   5   4   7   6   8   1

2   A gardener measured the heights of a group of plants.
   The heights were as follows.

   50 cm     65 cm     80 cm
   40 cm     35 cm

   Find the mean height.

3   In a test the marks were as follows.

   9   7   8   7   5   6   8   9   5   6

   Find the mean mark.

4   The ages of a group of friends are as follows.

   18   22   21   19   18
   18   17   19   17   21

   Find the mean age.

5   The salaries of ten workers in a small company are as follows.

   £20 000      £20 000
   £20 000      £18 000
   £22 000      £23 000
   £25 000      £21 000
   £23 000      £28 000

   Find the mean salary.

# EXERCISE 43.4H

1   Find the range of this set of data.

   3   6   5   4   7   6   8   1

2   A gardener measured the heights of a group of plants.
   The heights were as follows.

   50 cm     65 cm     80 cm
   40 cm     35 cm

   Find the range of the heights.

3   In a test the marks were as follows.

   9   7   8   7   5   6   8   9   5   6

   Find the range of the marks.

4   The ages of a group of friends are as follows.

   18   22   21   19   18
   18   17   19   17   21

   Find the range of their ages.

5   The salaries of ten workers in a small company are as follows.

   £20 000      £20 000
   £20 000      £18 000
   £22 000      £23 000
   £25 000      £21 000
   £23 000      £28 000

   Find the range of their salaries.

# EXERCISE 43.5H

1　This table shows the weights of the women in a keep fit group.

| Weight in kg (to the nearest kilogram) | Number of members |
|---|---|
| 45–49 | 8 |
| 50–54 | 12 |
| 55–59 | 10 |
| 60–64 | 6 |
| 65–69 | 8 |

Write down the modal class.

2　This table shows the weekly pay of 30 workers.

| Weekly pay (£) | Number of members |
|---|---|
| 100–149.99 | 3 |
| 150–199.99 | 10 |
| 200–249.99 | 12 |
| 249–300.99 | 5 |

Write down the modal class.

3　The ages of the people at a bridge club are shown in this table.

| Age | Number of people |
|---|---|
| 20–29 | 5 |
| 30–39 | 12 |
| 40–49 | 8 |
| 50–59 | 15 |
| 60–69 | 26 |
| 70–79 | 10 |

Find the modal class.

4　The marks gained in a test are shown below.

| | | | | |
|---|---|---|---|---|
| 55 | 60 | 62 | 74 | 53 |
| 59 | 73 | 81 | 91 | 48 |
| 43 | 62 | 90 | 85 | 45 |
| 63 | 67 | 75 | 49 | 84 |
| 61 | 67 | 44 | 68 | 77 |
| 83 | 49 | 84 | 76 | 63 |
| 53 | 73 | 88 | 64 | 74 |
| 79 | 56 | 63 | 44 | 59 |
| 82 | 59 | 65 | 57 | 87 |
| 83 | 72 | 70 | 51 | 48 |

Copy and complete the frequency table and write down the modal class.

| Mark | Tally | Total |
|---|---|---|
| 41–50 | | |
| 51–60 | | |
| 61–70 | | |
| 71–80 | | |
| 81–90 | | |
| 91–100 | | |

# REVIEW EXERCISE 43H

**1** The marks obtained by Jane in nine mathematics tests are

78   67   75   89   86
46   66   78   84

Calculate the mean value of these marks.

**2** Anika plays golf, her scores in her recent matches are

75   74   69   83   79   82   65
87   75   73   71   74   81

**a)** Find the range of the scores.

**b)** Find the mean value of these scores.

**3** Samantha is preparing for a holiday. She looks up the cost of the same holiday in a number of different brochures. The costs are shown below.

£320   £365   £299   £405
£354   £387   £368   £310

**a)** Find the range of these costs.

**b)** Find the mean value of these costs.

**4** The scores obtained by a player in eleven games of cricket are shown below.

15   0   35   2   56   2
75   5   21   2   17

**a)** Write down the mode for these scores.

**b)** Find the median value of the scores.

**5** 7 4 7 5 5 6 7 8 7 8 4 7 4 3 5

For the numbers shown above

**a)** find the median.

**b)** write down the mode.

**c)** find the range.

**d)** calculate the mean value.

**6** 23 35 33 26 53 28 45 35 18 44

For the numbers shown above

**a)** write down the range of the numbers.

**b)** calculate the mean value of the numbers.

**7** 1 3 7 4 2 9 8 7 2 6 2 8 2 9 9

For the numbers shown above, write down

**a)** the mode.

**b)** the median.

**8** The numbers of computer games sold per day by a shop in the nine days before Christmas were as follows.

23   34   45   35   65
56   39   54   63

**a)** What is the range of the number of computer games sold per day?

**b)** Calculate the mean number of computer games sold per day.

**9** When the spinner shown below is spun, it is equally likely to land on any of the numbers shown.

Wendy spins the above spinner thirteen times. Her results are as follows.

1    3    3    5    4    2    6
6    4    5    5    3    3

For these values, write down
**a)** the mode.
**b)** the median.

## EXERCISE 44.1H

1  The pictogram shows the number of customers buying pizzas in a takeaway restaurant one week.
   a) How many pizzas were sold on Tuesday?
   b) How many pizzas were sold on the busiest day?
   c) How many pizzas were sold in the week?
   d) What is the mean number of pizzas sold each day?

◎ represents 20 sales

| Monday | ◎◎◎ |
|---|---|
| Tuesday | ◎◎◎ |
| Wednesday | ◎◎◎ |
| Thursday | ◎◎◎ |
| Friday | ◎◎◎◎◎ |
| Saturday | ◎◎◎◎◎◎◎ |
| Sunday | ◎◎◎◎ |

2  The pictogram shows the number of people attending a skating rink one week.
   a) Which days were least popular for skating?
   b) How many skaters were there on Wednesday?
   c) How many skaters were there in the week?
   d) What is the mean number of skaters each day?

■ represents 40 skaters

| Monday | ■■ |
|---|---|
| Tuesday | ■■ |
| Wednesday | ■■■ |
| Thursday | ■■■ |
| Friday | ■■ |
| Saturday | ■■■■■ |
| Sunday | ■■■■■■ |

3  The pictogram shows the number of parasols sold by a garden centre one year.
   a) How many parasols did the garden centre sell in summer?
   b) How many parasols did the garden centre sell in the year?
   c) What is the mean number of parasols sold each *month*?

● represents 1000 parasols

| Spring | ●◗ |
|---|---|
| Summer | ●●●◗ |
| Autumn | ◖ |
| Winter | ◢ |

**4** The pictogram shows the number of cucumbers sold by a greengrocer one week.

    **a)** Which day of the week was the greengrocer closed?

    **b)** How many cucumbers were sold on Thursday?

    **c)** How many cucumbers were sold in the week?

● represents 20 cucumbers

| Monday | ◣ |
|---|---|
| Tuesday | ◖ |
| Wednesday | ● ◖ |
| Thursday | ● |
| Friday | ● ◖ |
| Saturday | ● ● |

**5** The pictogram shows the number of drivers caught speeding by a speed camera one week.

    **a)** How many people were caught speeding on Wednesday?

    **b)** How many people were caught speeding on Monday?

    **c)** How many people were caught speeding in the week?

    **d)** What is the mean number of people caught speeding each day?

● represents 8 people

| Monday | ● ● ● ● ◖ |
|---|---|
| Tuesday | ● ● ◖ |
| Wednesday | ● ● ● |
| Thursday | ● ● ● ◖ |
| Friday | ● ● ● ● ● ◣ |
| Saturday | ● ● ● ◖ |
| Sunday | ● ● ◣ |

**6** The pictogram shows the number of televisions sold by a shop one year.

    **a)** How many televisions were sold in April?

    **b)** How many televisions are sold in the month with the least sales?

    **c)** How many televisions were sold in the year?

    **d)** What is the mean number of televisions sold each month?

▢ represents 4 televisions

| January | ▢ ▢ ▢ ▢ |
|---|---|
| February | ▢ ▢ ▢ ◖ |
| March | ▢ ▢ ▢ |
| April | ▢ ▢ ▢ ◖ |
| May | ▢ ▢ ▢ ◣ |
| June | ▢ ▢ ◣ |
| July | ▢ ▢ ◖ |
| August | ▢ ▢ ◣ |
| September | ▢ ▢ ▢ ◖ |
| October | ▢ ▢ ▢ |
| November | ▢ ▢ ▢ ◖ |
| December | ▢ ▢ ▢ ◣ |

# EXERCISE 44.2H

**1** The pie chart shows the favourite crisp flavour of 60 people questioned in a survey.

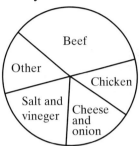

How many people preferred
**a)** beef?
**b)** cheese and onion?
**c)** salt and vinegar?

**2** The pie chart shows the eye colour of 108 people questioned in a survey.

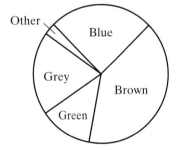

How many people had
**a)** blue eyes?    **b)** grey eyes?

**3** The pie chart shows the distribution of the population of Britain.

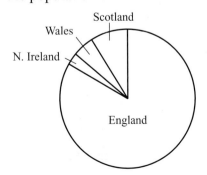

The total population of Britain is approximately 60 million people.
What is the approximate population of
**a)** England?    **b)** Scotland?
**c)** Northern Ireland?
**d)** Wales?

**4** The pie chart shows the approximate land area of Britain.

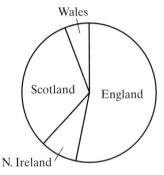

The total land area of Britain is approximately 94 320 square miles.
What is the approximate land area of
**a)** England?    **b)** Wales?
**c)** Northern Ireland?
**d)** Scotland?

**5** The pie chart shows the ingredients needed to make fruit crumble.

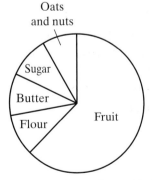

Betty makes a large fruit crumble weighing 2.4 kg.
What is the approximate weight, in grams, of each of the ingredients of Betty's crumble?

# EXERCISE 44.3H

1   The temperature of some water was taken every 5 minutes as it was heated. The line graph shows the results.

a)   What was the temperature of the water before it was heated?
b)   How many minutes did it take for the liquid to reach 75°C?
c)   By how many degrees did the water temperature rise in the first 20 minutes?
d)   What happened after 30 minutes?

2   The line graph shows the number of spectators at the first six games played by Rangers and by Rovers in the season.

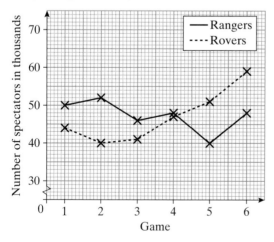

a)   How big was the crowd for at Rovers' second game?
b)   For which game did both teams have approximately the same size crowd?
c)   What was the range of the crowd size for the Rangers games?
d)   What was the mean crowd size for the Rovers games?
e)   Can you use this information to predict crowd sizes for game 7? Explain your answer.

3   The line graph below shows the total rainfall in Bananaland theme park one year.

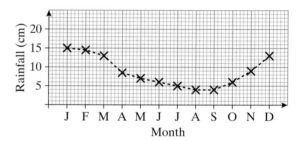

a)   How much rain fell in June?
b)   Which month had the most rain?
c)   What was the range of the monthly rainfall figures for the year?
d)   Calculate the mean monthly rainfall for the year.

**4**  The line graph shows the value of sales of a mushroom farm one year.

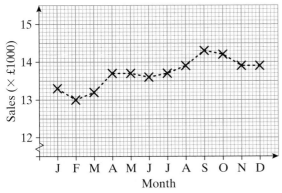

a) Which month had the lowest sales?
b) What was the range of sales values for the year?
c) What was the total value of sales for the year?
d) What was the mean value of sales each month?

**5**  The line graph shows the number of drivers paying to cross a toll bridge one week.

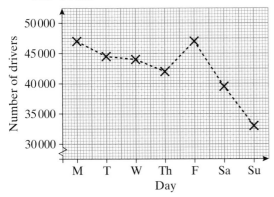

a) How many drivers crossed the bridge during the week?
b) What was the mean number of drivers crossing the bridge each day?
c) What was the range of the number of drivers crossing the bridge each day?
d) Why might there be fewer drivers crossing the bridge on Saturday and Sunday?

**6**  The line graph shows the mean monthly rainfall and maximum daily temperature in Brisbane one year.

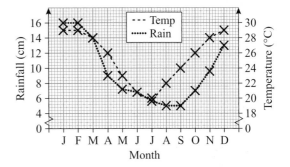

a) Which months had the highest mean monthly rainfall?
b) Which months had the highest maximum daily temperature?
c) What was the maximum daily temperature in September?
d) In which month was the mean monthly rainfall approximately 14 cm?
e) What was the range of the maximum daily temperature for the year?
f) What was the range of the mean monthly rainfall for the year?

# EXERCISE 44.4H

1   The pie charts show the number of
    companies involved in the automotive
    trade in the UK in 2007 and 2009.
    The total number of companies in each
    year was the same.

**Number of companies in 2007**

**Number of companies in 2009**

a)  In which year was the number of
    car repair companies larger?
b)  What is the main difference
    between the two years?
c)  What similarities are there between
    the two years?

2   The bar charts show the marks
    obtained by boys and girls in a general
    knowledge test.

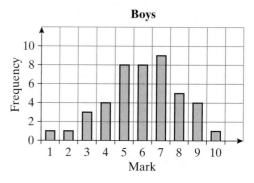

a)  How many girls scored 7 in the test?
b)  How many boys scored 4 in the test?
c)  What was the modal score for the
    girls?
d)  What was the modal score for the
    boys?
e)  What was the range of the scores
    for the girls?
f)  Did girls or boys do better in this
    test?
    Give a reason for your answer.

**3** One measure of the health of a country is its Infant Mortality Rate (IMR). The bar charts below show the IMR of five developed and five undeveloped countries.

**Developed**

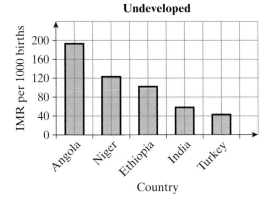

**Undeveloped**

**a)** Approximately, what is the IMR of the UK?

**b)** Approximately, what is the IMR of Angola?

**c)** Approximately, what is the mean IMR for the undeveloped countries?

**d)** Approximately, what is the mean IMR for the developed countries?

**e)** Approximately, what is the range of the IMRs for all 10 countries?

**f)** Which group of countries is the healthiest?

**g)** Draw a bar chart to show the data for all ten countries.

## EXERCISE 45.1H

1   For a project, Rebecca recorded the ages of 100 cars as they passed the school gates one morning. Here are her results.

| Age (a years) | $0 \leqslant a < 2$ | $2 \leqslant a < 4$ | $4 \leqslant a < 6$ | $6 \leqslant a < 8$ | $8 \leqslant a < 10$ | $10 \leqslant a < 12$ | $12 \leqslant a < 14$ |
|---|---|---|---|---|---|---|---|
| Frequency | 16 | 23 | 24 | 17 | 12 | 7 | 1 |

   a)   Draw a frequency diagram to show these data.
   b)   Which of the intervals is the modal class?

2   The manager of a leisure centre recorded the weights of 120 men. Here are the results.

| Weight (w kg) | $60 \leqslant w < 65$ | $65 \leqslant w < 70$ | $70 \leqslant w < 75$ | $75 \leqslant w < 80$ | $80 \leqslant w < 85$ | $85 \leqslant w < 90$ |
|---|---|---|---|---|---|---|
| Frequency | 4 | 18 | 36 | 50 | 10 | 2 |

   a)   Draw a frequency diagram to represent these data.
   b)   Which of the intervals is the modal class?
   c)   Which of the intervals contains the median value?

3   This frequency diagram shows the times taken by a group of girls to run a race.
   a)   How many girls took longer than 9 minutes?
   b)   How many girls took part in the race?
   c)   What percentage of the girls took less than 7 minutes?
   d)   What is the modal finishing time?
   e)   Use the diagram to draw up a grouped frequency table like those in questions **1** and **2**.

# EXERCISE 45.2H

1    The table shows the heights of 40 plants.

| Height ($h$ cm) | $3 \leqslant h < 4$ | $4 \leqslant h < 5$ | $5 \leqslant h < 6$ | $6 \leqslant h < 7$ | $7 \leqslant h < 8$ | $8 \leqslant h < 9$ |
|---|---|---|---|---|---|---|
| Frequency | 1 | 7 | 10 | 12 | 8 | 2 |

Draw a frequency polygon to show these data.

2    The table shows the time taken for a group of children to get from home to school.

| Time ($t$ mins) | $0 \leqslant t < 5$ | $5 \leqslant t < 10$ | $10 \leqslant t < 15$ | $15 \leqslant t < 20$ | $20 \leqslant t < 25$ | $25 \leqslant t < 30$ |
|---|---|---|---|---|---|---|
| Frequency | 3 | 15 | 27 | 34 | 19 | 2 |

Draw a frequency polygon to show these data.

3    The ages of all of the people under 70 in a small village were recorded in 1989 and 2009.
The results are given in the table below.

| Age ($a$ years) | $0 \leqslant a < 10$ | $10 \leqslant a < 20$ | $20 \leqslant a < 30$ | $30 \leqslant a < 40$ | $40 \leqslant a < 50$ | $50 \leqslant a < 60$ | $60 \leqslant a < 70$ |
|---|---|---|---|---|---|---|---|
| Frequency 1985 | 85 | 78 | 70 | 53 | 40 | 28 | 18 |
| Frequency 2005 | 50 | 51 | 78 | 76 | 62 | 64 | 56 |

a)   On the same grid, draw a frequency polygon for each year.
b)   Use the diagram to compare the distribution of ages in the two years.

# EXERCISE 45.3H

1   Bill grows tomatoes. As an experiment, he divided his land into eight plots.
    He used a different amount of fertiliser on each plot.
    The table shows the weight of tomatoes he got from each of the plots.

| Amount of fertiliser (g/m²) | 10 | 20 | 30 | 40 | 50 | 60 | 70 | 80 |
|---|---|---|---|---|---|---|---|---|
| Weight of tomatoes (kg) | 36 | 41 | 58 | 60 | 70 | 76 | 75 | 92 |

   a)  Draw a scatter diagram to show this information.
   b)  Describe the correlation shown in the scatter diagram.
   c)  The mean of the amount of fertiliser is 45 g/m². Calculate the mean weight of the
       tomatoes.
   d)  Plot the point that has these means as coordinates.
   e)  Draw a line of best fit on your scatter diagram.
   f)  What weight of tomatoes should Bill expect to get if he used 75 g/m²?

2   The table shows the prices and mileages of seven second-hand cars of the same model.

| Price (£) | 6000 | 3500 | 1000 | 8500 | 5500 | 3500 | 7000 |
|---|---|---|---|---|---|---|---|
| Mileage | 29 000 | 69 000 | 92 000 | 17 000 | 53 000 | 82 000 | 43 000 |

   a)  Draw a scatter diagram to show this information.
   b)  Describe the correlation shown in the scatter diagram.
   c)  The mean price is £5000. Calculate the mean mileage.
   d)  Plot the point that has these means as coordinates.
   e)  Draw a line of best fit on your scatter diagram.
   f)  Use your line of best fit to estimate
       (i)   the price of this model of car with a mileage of 18 000 miles.
       (ii)  the mileage of this model of car which costs £4000.

3   The heights of 10 daughters, all aged 20, and their fathers are given in the table below.

| Height of father (cm) | 167 | 168 | 169 | 171 | 172 | 172 | 174 | 175 | 176 | 182 |
|---|---|---|---|---|---|---|---|---|---|---|
| Height of daughter (cm) | 164 | 166 | 166 | 168 | 169 | 170 | 170 | 171 | 173 | 177 |

   a)  Draw a scatter diagram to show this information.
   b)  Describe the correlation shown in the scatter diagram.
   c)  The mean height of the fathers is 172.6 cm. Calculate the mean height of the daughters.
   d)  Plot the point that has these means as coordinates.
   e)  Draw a line of best fit on your scatter diagram.
   f)  Use your line of best fit to estimate the height of a 20-year-old daughter whose
       father is 180 cm tall.

## EXERCISE 46.1H

1   For each of these sets of data
    (i) find the mode. (ii) find the median. (iii) find the range. (iv) calculate the mean.

a)

| Score on biased dice | Number of times thrown |
|---|---|
| 1 | 52 |
| 2 | 46 |
| 3 | 70 |
| 4 | 54 |
| 5 | 36 |
| 6 | 42 |
| Total | 300 |

b)

| Number of drawing pins in a box | Number of boxes |
|---|---|
| 98 | 5 |
| 99 | 14 |
| 100 | 36 |
| 101 | 28 |
| 102 | 17 |
| 103 | 13 |
| 104 | 7 |
| Total | 120 |

c)

| Number of snacks per day | Frequency |
|---|---|
| 0 | 23 |
| 1 | 68 |
| 2 | 39 |
| 3 | 21 |
| 4 | 10 |
| 5 | 3 |
| 6 | 1 |

d)

| Number of letters received on Monday | Frequency |
|---|---|
| 0 | 19 |
| 1 | 37 |
| 2 | 18 |
| 3 | 24 |
| 4 | 12 |
| 5 | 5 |
| 6 | 2 |
| 7 | 3 |

**2** Gift tokens cost £1, £5, £10, £20 or £50 each.
The frequency table below shows the numbers of each value of gift token sold in one bookstore on a Saturday.
Calculate the mean value of gift token bought in the bookstore that Saturday.

| Price of gift token (£) | 1 | 5 | 10 | 20 | 50 |
|---|---|---|---|---|---|
| Number of tokens sold | 12 | 34 | 26 | 9 | 1 |

**3** A sample of people were asked how many visits to the cinema they had made in one month.
None of those asked had made more than eight visits to the cinema.
The table below shows the data.
Calculate the mean number of visits to the cinema.

| Number of visits | 0 | 1 | 2 | 3 | 4 | 5 | 6 | 7 | 8 |
|---|---|---|---|---|---|---|---|---|---|
| Frequency | 136 | 123 | 72 | 41 | 18 | 0 | 5 | 1 | 4 |

# EXERCISE 46.2H

**1** For each of these sets of data, calculate an estimate of
   **(i)** the range.    **(ii)** the mean.

a)

| Number of trains arriving late each day (x) | Number of days (f) |
|---|---|
| 0–4 | 19 |
| 5–9 | 9 |
| 10–14 | 3 |
| 15–19 | 0 |
| 20–24 | 1 |
| Total | 32 |

b)

| Number of weeds per square metre (x) | Number of square metres (f) |
|---|---|
| 0–14 | 204 |
| 15–29 | 101 |
| 30–44 | 39 |
| 45–59 | 13 |
| 60–74 | 6 |
| 75–89 | 2 |

**c)**

| Number of books sold (x) | Frequency (f) |
|---|---|
| 60–64 | 3 |
| 65–69 | 12 |
| 70–74 | 23 |
| 75–79 | 9 |
| 80–84 | 4 |
| 85–89 | 1 |

**d)**

| Number of days absent (x) | Frequency (f) |
|---|---|
| 0–3 | 13 |
| 4–7 | 18 |
| 8–11 | 9 |
| 12–15 | 4 |
| 16–19 | 0 |
| 20–23 | 1 |
| 24–27 | 3 |

**2** The table below gives the number of sentences per chapter in a book.

| Number of sentences (x) | $100 \leqslant x < 125$ | $125 \leqslant x < 150$ | $150 \leqslant x < 175$ | $175 \leqslant x < 200$ | $200 \leqslant x < 225$ |
|---|---|---|---|---|---|
| Frequency | 1 | 9 | 8 | 5 | 2 |

a) What is the modal class?
b) In which group is the median number of sentences?
c) Calculate an estimate of the mean number of sentences.

**3** A group of students were asked to estimate the number of beans in a jar.
The results of their estimates are summarised in the table.
Calculate an estimate of the mean number of beans estimated by these students.

| Estimated number of beans (x) | Frequency (f) |
|---|---|
| 300–324 | 9 |
| 325–349 | 26 |
| 350–374 | 52 |
| 375–399 | 64 |
| 400–424 | 83 |
| 425–449 | 57 |
| 450–474 | 18 |
| 475–499 | 5 |

# EXERCISE 46.3H

1  For each of these sets of data, calculate an estimate of
   (i)  the range.                    (ii)  the mean.

a)

| Height of sunflower in centimetres ($x$) | Number of plants ($f$) |
|---|---|
| $100 \leqslant x < 110$ | 6 |
| $110 \leqslant x < 120$ | 13 |
| $120 \leqslant x < 130$ | 35 |
| $130 \leqslant x < 140$ | 29 |
| $140 \leqslant x < 150$ | 16 |
| $150 \leqslant x < 160$ | 11 |
| Total | 110 |

b)

| Weight of egg in grams ($x$) | Number of eggs ($f$) |
|---|---|
| $20 \leqslant x < 25$ | 9 |
| $25 \leqslant x < 30$ | 16 |
| $30 \leqslant x < 35$ | 33 |
| $35 \leqslant x < 40$ | 48 |
| $40 \leqslant x < 45$ | 29 |
| $45 \leqslant x < 50$ | 15 |
| Total | 150 |

c)

| Length of green bean in millimetres ($x$) | Frequency ($f$) |
|---|---|
| $60 \leqslant x < 80$ | 12 |
| $80 \leqslant x < 100$ | 21 |
| $100 \leqslant x < 120$ | 46 |
| $120 \leqslant x < 140$ | 27 |
| $140 \leqslant x < 160$ | 14 |
| Total | 120 |

d)

| Time to complete race in minutes ($x$) | Frequency ($f$) |
|---|---|
| $54 \leqslant x < 56$ | 1 |
| $56 \leqslant x < 58$ | 4 |
| $58 \leqslant x < 60$ | 11 |
| $60 \leqslant x < 62$ | 6 |
| $62 \leqslant x < 64$ | 2 |
| $64 \leqslant x < 66$ | 1 |
| Total | 25 |

2  For each of these sets of data
   (i)  write down the modal class.          (ii)  calculate an estimate of the mean.

a)

| Height of shrub in metres ($x$) | Number of shrubs ($f$) |
|---|---|
| $0.3 \leqslant x < 0.6$ | 57 |
| $0.6 \leqslant x < 0.9$ | 41 |
| $0.9 \leqslant x < 1.2$ | 36 |
| $1.2 \leqslant x < 1.5$ | 24 |
| $1.5 \leqslant x < 1.8$ | 15 |

b)

| Weight of plum in grams ($x$) | Number of plums ($f$) |
|---|---|
| $20 \leqslant x < 30$ | 6 |
| $30 \leqslant x < 40$ | 19 |
| $40 \leqslant x < 50$ | 58 |
| $50 \leqslant x < 60$ | 15 |
| $60 \leqslant x < 70$ | 4 |

**c)**

| Length of journey in minutes (x) | Frequency (f) |
|---|---|
| $20 \leqslant x < 22$ | 6 |
| $22 \leqslant x < 24$ | 20 |
| $24 \leqslant x < 26$ | 38 |
| $26 \leqslant x < 28$ | 47 |
| $28 \leqslant x < 30$ | 16 |
| $30 \leqslant x < 32$ | 3 |

**d)**

| Speed of car in miles per hour (x) | Frequency (f) |
|---|---|
| $25 \leqslant x < 30$ | 4 |
| $30 \leqslant x < 35$ | 29 |
| $35 \leqslant x < 40$ | 33 |
| $40 \leqslant x < 45$ | 6 |
| $45 \leqslant x < 50$ | 2 |
| $50 \leqslant x < 55$ | 1 |

**3** The table shows the monthly wages of the workers in an office.

| Wages in £ (x) | $500 \leqslant x < 1000$ | $1000 \leqslant x < 1500$ | $1500 \leqslant x < 2000$ | $2000 \leqslant x < 2500$ |
|---|---|---|---|---|
| Frequency (f) | 3 | 14 | 18 | 5 |

a) What is the modal class?
b) In which class is the median wage?
c) Calculate an estimate of the mean wage.

**4** The table shows the length, in seconds, of 100 calls made from a mobile phone.

| Length of call in seconds (x) | $0 \leqslant x < 30$ | $30 \leqslant x < 60$ | $60 \leqslant x < 90$ | $90 \leqslant x < 120$ | $120 \leqslant x < 150$ |
|---|---|---|---|---|---|
| Frequency (f) | 51 | 25 | 13 | 7 | 4 |

Calculate an estimate of the mean length of a call.

**5** The table shows the prices paid for greetings cards sold in one day by a card shop.

Calculate an estimate of the mean price, in pence, paid for a greetings card that day.

| Price of greetings card in pence (x) | Frequency (f) |
|---|---|
| $75 \leqslant x < 100$ | 23 |
| $100 \leqslant x < 125$ | 31 |
| $125 \leqslant x < 150$ | 72 |
| $150 \leqslant x < 175$ | 59 |
| $175 \leqslant x < 200$ | 34 |
| $200 \leqslant x < 225$ | 11 |
| $225 \leqslant x < 250$ | 5 |

## EXERCISE 47.1H

1   State whether the following are primary data or secondary data.
    a)   Weighing packets of sweets
    b)   Using bus timetables
    c)   Looking up holiday prices on the internet
    d)   A GP entering data for a new patient on his records after seeing the patient

2   Lisa is doing a survey and has written this question.

> What colour is your hair?
>
> Black ☐   Brown ☐   Blonde ☐

   a)   Give a reason why this question is unsuitable.
   b)   Write a better version.

3   Steve is doing a survey about his local sports facilities.
    Here is one of his questions.

> How much do you enjoy doing sport?
>
>   1      2      3      4      5

   a)   Give a reason why this question is unsuitable.
   b)   Write a better version.

4   Mia is doing a survey about school lunches.
    She gives out questionnaires to the first 30 people in the queue for lunch.
    a)   Why is this likely to give a biased sample?
    b)   Describe a better method of obtaining a sample for her survey.

5   Here is one of Mia's questions.

> Don't you agree that we don't have enough salads on the menu?

   a)   Give a reason why this question is unsuitable.
   b)   Write a better version.

6   A survey is to be done about school students' earnings and pocket money. Write five suitable questions which should be included in such a survey.